D1605629

Apples
of
Gold

RAMON BENNETT

SHEKINAH

JERUSALEM – COLORADO SPRINGS

Copyright © 2017 Ramon Bennett
All Rights Reserved
First printed February 2017

ISBN 978-1-943423-21-7

Published in the United States by Shekinah Books LLC

Distributed in Israel by: Ramon Bennett,
P. O. Box 37111, Jerusalem 91370.
e-mail: armofsalvation@mac.com.

SHEKINAH

Shekinah Books LLC
A division of *Arm of Salvation Ministries,* Jerusalem.

This paperback is subject to discounts for orders of 10 or more copies when purchased through Shekinah Books. *Apples of Gold* is also available as a Kindle e-Book or in PDF form. Further information can be obtained, and purchases of multiple hard copies or single PDF purchases may be made, by logging onto: *http://www.shekinahbooks.com.*

A word fitly spoken is like apples of gold in settings of silver

(Proverbs 25:11).

For Ellie

Contents

Introduction

God created every human being individually. And
he gave each one individual gifts and individual
talents, which we are to use in his service;
however, many Christians seem only to amble through
life, producing little or nothing in the way of fruit for the
kingdom of God, and are satisfied to be taught Bible on
Sundays according to tradition, putting little effort into
gaining knowledge of the Most High for themselves.
Unfortunately, such Christians may be Bible-taught, but
they are not Spirit taught. For a Christian to understand
revealed truths it requires acts of the Holy Spirit equal
to the original that inspired the Scriptures, but we must
first have the essential ingredient—a real desire to seek
out scriptural truth.

I have had an insatiable love and a hunger for
God's word for over half a century. From the start of my
Christian walk I would read and reread the Bible from
cover to cover again and again and again, hours at a
time—I desire it more than my necessary food. As the
decades passed by I slowed down in the reading of so
much quantity in preference for reading more of quality.
I will often meditate on a verse of scripture, or part of a
verse, for hours, even days. I seem to have a gaping hole,
a huge vacuum in my innermost being that cries out to
be filled with the knowledge of God Almighty and of his
Son, Jesus; I have found that the knowledge of the One
leads to the knowledge of the Other.

God chose to give me a gift; that of an inquisitive, analytical mind, a mind that asks "Why?" about almost everything. This has probably created for me as many antagonists as it has friends.

Both Christians and non-Christians will often parrot something they have been told or taught without so much as questioning the veracity of it, whether it is in fact true or not. Some people, including Christians, most politicians, many journalists, and just as many teachers, get defensive when faced with the question "Why?" after airing a particular offcut of information. This is usually because they do not have the answer to the question.

When approaching a doctrine or a dogma many Christians unconsciously wear blinders (blinkers) like a horse, seeing only what is immediately before them and not the wider picture. Of a consequence their Bible knowledge is often restricted or skewed.

Christians should always be aware of the fact that only God is infallible. Even the greatest, the most gifted and the most learned of Christian scholars among us (and those who have lived throughout the ages), are and were human, therefore they are or were fallible. None were or are finite, and none of the monumental scholarly works that man has labored over and left for posterity can be said to be infallible. There is and always will be room for improvement in our understanding of Bible truth.

Noted translator and teacher William Barclay wrote:

> The Church is full of people who think that there is no way of doing things but their way. To change a customary or traditional way of doing things is worse

than heresy. But the way of doing things that annoys us may be the way of doing things which brings salvation to someone else's soul!

Thirty-six years ago I enrolled in an *ulpan* (Hebrew-language school) for beginners in Tel Aviv, Israel. After three months of group tuition I had learned just about enough Hebrew to begin asking "*lama?*" (Why?) about certain things. More often than not the answer I received was, "*kahah*" (that's how it is). To me this was unacceptable; there had to be reasons and rules, even in the Hebrew language.

One particular day in class the teacher introduced her students to the word, אצל (*etzel*), which seemed to have no clear meaning in the context of its use in the Hebrew sentence: "I ate *etzel* mother." We were given to understand that it meant "near," or "at the side of." Of course, I asked of the teacher, "*lama?* Why use this word; what is its origin?" Obviously, having already begun to lose patience with me, her answer was a short, blunt "*kahah* Ramon!" It was around this time that I understood that probably most Hebrew-language teachers could teach the language, knew the rules of grammar, etc., but did not know Hebrew etymology beyond the basics. And no native Hebrew-speaker I met in the immediate days following could explain the word *etzel* to me either.

At that time I was studying the book of Genesis in my times alone with the Lord and was pursuing my endeavor to know Hebrew by doing a verse-by-verse comparison between an English-language translation and the original Hebrew text. I was reading the passage in Genesis concerning the two angels that came to Sodom and who were taken by Lot into his house for the night. Most Christian readers will know how the story unfolds: a crowd of sodomites—male homosexuals—demanded of Lot that he give the angels to them for sex. In response, Lot says:

*See now, I have two daughters who have not known a man; please, let me bring them out to you, and **you may do to them as you wish; only do nothing to these men**, since this is the reason they have come **under the shadow of my roof** (Genesis 19:8).*

When I read the verse in Hebrew, it was as if a bolt of lightening struck the room! In Hebrew, the verse reads:

נא אתהן אליכם ועשו להן כטוב בעיניכם רק
הנה-נא לי שתי בנות אשר לא-ידעו איש אוציאה
לאנשים האל אל-תעשו דבר כי-על-כן **באו בצל קרתי**

Suddenly I knew the origin of the word *etzel*, and the true meaning of it.

Hebrew is read from right to left, and the next to last word in the above Hebrew text is בצל (*b'tzel*), which literally translates as "in the shadow." Therefore, the original meaning of אצל (*etzel*) meant so much more than "near," or "at the side of." In yesteryear, "I ate *etzel* mother" in Hebrew would literally have meant "I ate in the shadow of my mother." A more exact representation would be, "I ate under the protection of my mother," which is completely different to today's modern meaning of the word.

In the Genesis narrative Lot shows us the strength of the word's original meaning, and this should profoundly affect each of our personal relationships with our Heavenly Father.

Lot was prepared to give his two virgin daughters to be sexually abused and ravaged by a homosexual mob rather than give his guests, who were in his house, under his protection, over to the sodomites. The biblical word אצל (*etzel*) literally means that those inviting others into their homes for whatever reason, were **totally responsible for those in their care** and were obliged to do everything within their power to protect the ones under their roof no matter what the personal cost might be. This should be an immense encouragement to all true believers for:

He who dwells in the secret place of the Most High **shall abide under the shadow of the Almighty** (Psalms 91:1).

Which means to say that when a person receives Jesus and is truly born-again, that person becomes a child of God and comes under his care and protection. God, who does not change (Malachi 3:6)—with whom there is never the slightest variation or shadow of inconsistency (James 1:17)—becomes absolutely responsible for his new child. Surely this must dispel any and every concern that twice-born believers in Jesus may have about the future.

The discovery of the real meaning of אצל (*etzel*) gave me added impetus to study the word of the Living God in Hebrew each day more intensely. Over the years many truths began to open up to me through the Holy Spirit.

Three months following my first discovery in the Hebrew Bible I relocated to Jerusalem; there I enrolled in another *ulpan*. However, the inevitable *kahah!* in response to my *lama?* caused me to be so disillusioned with the teaching that I gave up the study of spoken Hebrew and opened up a business that produced custom furniture and cabinetry instead.

Some five years later I was introduced to the then 86-year-old Dola Ben-Yehuda Whitman, Eliezer Ben-Yehuda's youngest daughter and at that time one of the only two surviving Ben-Yehuda children. (Eliezer Ben-Yehuda was the man used by God to restore Hebrew into the vernacular language now spoken in Israel. Ben-Yehuda would not allow any of his nine children to play with other children, or to even hear other "filthy languages," as he termed all other tongues. No guests were ever allowed into the Ben-Yehuda home unless they first swore, on pain of expulsion from the house, to speak only Hebrew). After a short conversation with Dola she offered to be my private Hebrew tutor.

I was ecstatic! Dola knew every word in the entire Hebrew language. She had completed her father's famous seventeen-volume Hebrew dictionary, and I was soon to learn there was no *lama?* that Dola could not give an immediate explanation for. We became much more than student and teacher, we were friends who visited each other long after tuition days had ended. Dola presented me with her last copy of her famous book, *The Tongue of the Prophets*, which is the riveting, incredible story of the Ben-Yehuda family and the restoration of the Hebrew language. On the flyleaf Dola inscribed in Hebrew: "To Ramon, my outstanding student from New Zealand." It is a book that I shall forever treasure.

At the beginning of this Introduction I said that people often parrot things they have been taught or told without so much as questioning whether it is true. Unfortunately, Christians are among the worst offenders. Many Christians hold to doctrines and beliefs they do not understand. They can neither explain them to themselves in private nor to others in public. A Christian should understand what he or she believes, and why. Christians should also understand that it is legitimate and necessary to question their beliefs in order to understand what they do actually believe. Oswald Chambers put it very succinctly in the daily devotional *Still Higher For His Highest* when he says that **"we need to beware of the ban of finality about our present views."** To that I would add, "Once a person has made up his mind about a particular doctrine or belief, no further light on it will come to him."

Some Christians will not even deem to read Bible commentaries, holding to the misapplied belief in John 16:13, which says the Spirit of truth will teach them. Fifty years ago I traveled down that road, but I learnt that God uses other brains besides our own in our learning process. Today I own numerous commentaries and reference books. I am very interested in what others have learned from their studies. A pithy quote from John Wooden says it all: **"It's what you learn after you know it all that counts."** That gem also applies to Bible students.

When a person is about to eat a meal of fish, he would be foolish indeed to throw away the fish meat simply because there are bones in it. A wise person will eat the meat of the fish with care, placing the bones on the side of the plate. And that is how Christians with teachable spirits should approach all commentaries, references, and other Christian books, including this one.

In these few brief pages I present some corrections that I believe are necessary to some popular Christian beliefs. Error has crept into both the Protestant and Catholic churches through inaccurate translation, or misunderstanding of the Hebrew and Greek texts. We also have the problem of tradition, which, along with prejudice, are the two things more powerful than fact. It is always easier to train a new Christian than to reprogram an old one. Some traditions are good and should be kept for time immemorial; some should be buried deep and never exhumed.

I also address a few popular misconceptions that are held by many Christians because tradition has always had it so. And I include some pages on well-known but little understood passages.

These short studies are offered along with a prayer that the reader, the average Bible student, will not only be edified, but will also be encouraged to *search the Scriptures* to see whether these things are so (Acts 17:11). Eat the meat and place the bones on the side of the plate, and bear in mind more of what William Barclay wrote:

> **It is a paradox that, unless a man is prepared to run the risk of being a heretic, he has little chance of arriving at the truth.**

In this small volume I shall touch upon some simple, non-controversial passages; however, some readers will surely regard one or two chapters to be very controversial because of traditional teachings. Do not be too quick to label those with a different view of a particular Christian belief as a heretic. The definition of heresy is **"an opinion or belief at odds with what is generally taught."** Surely a person is within his rights to challenge what is traditionally taught providing he can back it up with Scripture without having taken it out of context. Those that are familiar with my writings know that I make no attempts to be a people pleaser, nor do I live in fear of other people's reactions. I try only to please the One who gave his life so that I may live.

Many Christians *have become dull of hearing* and *need milk and not solid food* (Hebrews 5:11, 12); some of what I present in these pages is real *solid food*; those accustomed to *milk* may get indigestion.

Prayerfully consider all that I have written. If, after reading it, you feel some of your beliefs need tweaking or rethinking, adjust accordingly; eat the meat and place the bones on the side of the plate.

Readers may sound off at me by e-mail to the following address: *<ramon@shekinahbooks.com>*.

In The Spirit On The Lord's Day

I firmly believe one error in Church teaching is that John's vision on the isle of Patmos—where he had been banished for the crime of preaching Christ and the Word of God—took place on a Sunday, the Christian day of rest:

*It was **Sunday** and I was in the Spirit, praying. I heard a loud voice behind me, trumpet-clear and piercing*
(Revelation 1:10 *The Message*).

The great majority of translations render the verse thus:

*I was in the Spirit on **the Lord's day**, and I heard behind me a loud voice, as of a trumpet* (Revelation 1:10 *NKJV*).

Revelation 1:10 is the only time that the expression "*the Lord's day*" appears in the Bible. Some Christians in the first centuries of the Church held to the belief that the Lord's day was Good Friday, but over the years the Church consolidated the belief that Sunday, the first day of the week, should be dedicated to the Lord, and Sunday became recognized and spoken of as "the Lord's day."

Sunday being held as "the Lord's day" is merely another misguided tradition that runs contrary to biblical truth. This tradition is forced and reinforced into the minds of millions of Christians through Bible translations that contain traditional beliefs, translators' dogma and doctrines rather than biblical fact. The translation above of Revelation 1:10 from *The Message*, a popular modern Bible translation, is an example of tradition overriding fact.

That his vision took place on a Sunday is not at all what John meant to convey; this flawed teaching has given Christians throughout the ages a false perception regarding both Sunday and the Book of Revelation.

The Book of Revelation is also known by its original Greek title, Apocalypse, which is an obvious title to any student who has spent time in that Book. It is a far more appropriate title given today's understanding of the word apocalypse.

In Greek, the very first word of the Book of Revelation is Ἀποκάλυψις – *apocalypsis,* from which we get our English word apocalypse. Apocalypsis means "the uncovering of something hidden," and thus we arrive at our English title, *Revelation.*

Whereas the title "Apocalypse" strongly suggests to the reader that the subject of the book is doom-laden and catastrophic—which, in the main it is—the title *Revelation* steers us away from the cataclysmic subject-matter and leaves many modern Christians fixated upon Christ's letters to the seven churches found in Chapters 1 through 3: *Ephesus, Smyrna, Pergamos, Thyatira, Sardis, Philadelphia* and *Laodicea.*

At this point it should be made clear that the Book of *Revelation* is not John's revelation of Christ, it is Christ's revelation of what must shortly take place:

the revelation of Jesus Christ, **which God gave Him [Jesus] to show to His servants** *– things which must shortly take place...* (Revelation 1:1).

It is Almighty God revealing to us, through His Son, events that must take place in the future.

"*I was*" (Greek ἐγενόμην – *egenomēn*) means "*I came to be*" and at least one excellent translator does translate it so:

I came to be *in the Spirit on the Lord's day, and I heard behind me a great voice, as of a trumpet* (Revelation 1:10 *A Literal Translation of the Bible* by Jay P. Green Sr.).

However, I have only found one translation that captures the real intent and meaning of Revelation 1:10 and this is R.F. Weymouth's *The New Testament in Modern Speech*, that was first published in 1903. Weymouth translated the verse splendidly:

In the Spirit I found myself present on the day of the Lord, *and I heard behind me a loud voice which resembled the blast of a trumpet* (Revelation 1:10 *Weymouth*).

Weymouth comprehended John's intent and rendered it accordingly. Jay P. Green Sr. probably comprehended it also, but did not render it quite so vividly as Weymouth. The *Lord's Day* that John speaks of is none other than the great and terrible *Day of the* LORD, in which all nations and peoples are judged and destroyed except for the truly twice-born that have clung to Jesus through thick and thin, through many trials and tribulations. Jesus Himself says:

Because you have kept my command to persevere, I also will keep you from **the hour of trial which shall come upon the whole world**, *to test those who dwell on the earth* (Revelation 3:10).

The Day of the Lord is the terrible day of God's vengeance:

*The sun shall be turned into darkness, and the moon into blood, before the coming of the great and awesome **Day of the Lord*** (Acts 2:20).

Dear Lord:

Help us to be ready in mind and spirit for the coming of the great and awesome *Day of the Lord*. Help us to keep your commandments daily in this sick age in which we find ourselves living. Help us to commit our lives totally to you, and may you judge us worthy to be kept "*from the hour of trial that is coming upon the whole world*." Amen.

O Wretched Man that I Am

We should be aware that there are over four thousand fragments and pieces of codices from which the New Testament is made up. There are no extant whole codices and few almost whole manuscripts of a gospel or an epistle in existence. Adding to this difficulty is the fact that of the four thousand pieces of New Testament material there are no two identical written pieces, which obviously makes assembling and translating an accurate account of the New Testament a monumental task.

A particular text in Romans is one that I want to draw attention to; it is one that will ease the mind of many a reader and allow him or her to live in Christ in peace. A whole section is worth scrutiny and this is:

*For what I am doing, I do not understand. For **what I will to do, that I do not practice; but what I hate, that I do**. If, then, I do what I will not to do, I agree with the law that it is good. But now, it is no longer I who do it, but sin that dwells in me. For I know that in me (that is, in my flesh) nothing good dwells; for to will is present with me, but how to perform what is good I do not find. For **the good that I will to do, I do not do; but the evil I will not to do, that I practice**. Now if I do what I will not to do, it is no longer I who do it, but sin that dwells in me.*

I find then a law, that evil is present with me, the one who wills to do good. For I delight in the law of God according to the inward man. But I see another law in my members, warring against the law of my mind, and bringing me into captivity to the law of sin which is in my members. O wretched man that I am! **Who will deliver me from this body of death? I thank God—through Jesus Christ our Lord!**

So then, with the mind I myself serve the law of God, but with the flesh the law of sin.

There is therefore now no condemnation to those who are in Christ Jesus, who do not walk according to the flesh, but according to the Spirit. *For the law of the Spirit of life in Christ Jesus has made me free from the law of sin and death* (Romans 7:15 – 8:2).

The Greek word used for "*Who*" in the second paragraph of the above text is τίς (*tis*), an interrogative pronoun that is used five hundred and twenty-three times in the New Testament and means "who," "what," "which" and "why," as well as being translated as "whether," "wherefore," and "whereupon," but well over half of all the usages are as "What." Therefore, saying, "*Who* will deliver me from this body of death? I thank God through Jesus Christ our Lord!" gives us no answer to Paul's dilemma. I will come back to this scripture in a moment, but first let us take a look at another passage in Romans where the context surrounding "Who" is made very much clearer:

Who *shall separate us from the love of Christ? Shall* **tribulation, or distress, or persecution, or famine, or nakedness, or peril, or sword?** *…Yet in* **all these things** *we are more than conquerors through him who loved us. For I am persuaded that* **neither death nor life, nor angels nor principalities nor powers, nor things present nor things to come, nor height nor depth, nor any other**

created thing, *shall be able to separate us from the love of God which is in Christ Jesus our Lord*

(Romans 8:35, 37–39).

The "*Who*" in the immediate passage above is referring to "***things,***" and by no stretch of the imagination should "***things***" be addressed as "***who,***" so obviously we should be looking at:

What *shall separate us from the love of Christ? Shall* ***tribulation, or distress, or persecution, or famine, or nakedness, or peril, or sword?***

Paul's answer is that none of those "***things***" can. Therefore we come back to the Greek word τίς (*tis*), which means "what" and "why" as well as "who," and the context here is very much "***What,***" because it refers to "***things.***"

Going back now to Romans 7:24: ***Who*** *will deliver me from this body of death? I thank God through Jesus Christ our Lord!* We must first change "*Who*" and replace it with "*What,*" as in, ***What*** *will deliver me from this body of death?* And then we find there has to be a word missing in order to make perfect sense of the passage. The missing word must be a stand-alone word because it comes between "*death*?" and "*I thank God…,*" between a completed sentence and the beginning of a new one. There is only one possible word that would fit here and that is an emphatic, ***Grace!*** Therefore, Romans 7:24 should read: ***What*** *will deliver me from this body of death?* ***Grace!*** *I thank God through Jesus Christ our Lord!* Now the passage makes sense and Paul's words of feeling wretched become crystal clear, because *where sin abounded,* ***grace abounds*** *much more* (Romans 5:20).

The word "grace" is used one hundred and nineteen times throughout the New Testament, and John's gospel captures the true essence of grace:

For **the law was given through Moses, but grace and truth came through Jesus Christ** (John 1:17).

Paul wrote much about grace in his letter to the Romans—twenty-four times. Romans is the complete *gospel of the grace of God* (Acts 20:24)in a nutshell. Paul speaks about the Mosaic law, which is *the law of sin and death—**the soul that sins shall die*** (Ezekiel 18:4), but he argues that *the law of sin and death* is overruled by the law of *grace*:

*Moreover the law entered that the offense might abound. But where **sin abounded, grace abounded much more**, so that as sin reigned in death, even so **grace might reign through righteousness** to eternal life through Jesus Christ our Lord* (Romans 5:20–21).

In his letter to the Romans, Paul bares his heart and tells us that the good that he wants to do he does not do, and the bad things that he does not want to do are the very things that he does do; and that it is a "**wretched**" situation, then he supplies the answer:

What *will deliver me from this body of death?* **Grace!** *I thank God through Jesus Christ our Lord!* (Romans 7:25).

I mentioned that the New Testament has been pieced together from over four thousand fragments of codices. The best and most complete extant copy of Romans is Codex Sinaiticus, dated around the Fourth century, and is conserved in the Vatican Library. In the margin, next to the Romans 7:24 verse, there is an editor's note of "χάρις," (*charis*), that means "grace," "favor," "gratitude." The Fourth century editor picked up on the fact that the copyist had omitted the word and wrote it in the margin himself as an omitted word. Could the reason that Protestant New Testaments do not have the word included be because of tradition, the ridiculous aversion to all things Roman Catholic?

Whatever the reason may be, it was *Grace!* that would deliver Paul from his body of death and it is *grace* that will deliver us all from our own bodies of death. The last line of the third stanza of John Newton's famous hymn *Amazing Grace* says it all:

'tis *grace* that brought me safe thus far, and *grace* will lead me home.

Dear Lord:
Help us to understand that salvation and eternal life come solely by the grace of God. We cannot earn our redemption by any act other that repentance toward God and a firm belief in the Lord Jesus Christ. A firm belief of Jesus being the *Son of God* (Luke 1:35), who expressly came to offer up his life as *the Lamb of God that takes away the sin of the world* (John 1:29). Help us to realize that when we do stumble in our intimate walk with *the Light of the World* (John 8:12) and feel miserable as a result, that *Grace!* will deliver us from our *body of death* and it shall be *Grace!* that will lead us home into the arms of him who will wipe away *every tear from our eyes* (Revelation 21:4). Amen.

A People of Unclean Lips

Over the past fifty years I have heard a number of explanations for the prophet Isaiah's words, *"Woe is me, for I am undone! Because **I am a man of unclean lips, and I dwell in the midst of a people of unclean lips*** (Isaiah 6:5), but I do not believe any of these explanations have come near the true meaning of them.`Here is the full scripture passage that encompasses Isaiah's words and indicates the reason for them:

*In the year that **King Uzziah** died, I saw the Lord sitting on a throne, high and lifted up, and the train of his robe filled the temple. Above it stood seraphim; each one had six wings: with two he covered his face, with two he covered his feet, and with two he flew. And one cried to another and said: "Holy, holy, holy is the Lord of hosts; the whole earth is full of his glory!" And the posts of the door were shaken by the voice of him who cried out, and the house was filled with smoke. So I said: "Woe is me, for I am undone! Because **I am a man of unclean lips, and I dwell in the midst of a people of unclean lips**; for my eyes have seen the King, the Lord of hosts." Then one of the seraphim flew to me, having in his hand a live coal which he had taken with the tongs from the altar. And he touched my mouth with it, and said: "Behold, this has touched your lips; your iniquity is taken away, and your sin purged"* (Isaiah 6:1-7).

"In the year that King Uzziah died." For Isaiah to begin with these words tells us that they are important and

have a bearing on what will follow. Isaiah's first words provide the first clue—the key to unlocking the meaning of what Isaiah wanted to convey to his readers.

King Uzziah was a good king who built Israel's fighting forces into a fearsome army of men and machines; however, he was made a leper by God Almighty because he did what was not within his authority to do:

When Uzziah was strong his heart was lifted up, to his destruction, for he transgressed against the LORD his God by entering the temple of the LORD to burn incense on the altar of incense. So Azariah the priest went in after him, and with him were eighty priests of the LORD—valiant men. And they withstood King Uzziah, and said to him, "It is not for you, Uzziah, to burn incense to the LORD, but for the priests, the sons of Aaron, who are consecrated to burn incense. Get out of the sanctuary, for you have trespassed! You shall have no honor from the LORD God."

*Then Uzziah became furious; and he had a censer in his hand to burn incense. And while he was angry with the priests, **leprosy** broke out on his forehead, before the priests in the house of the LORD, beside the incense altar. And Azariah the chief priest and all the priests looked at him, and there, on his forehead, **he was leprous**; so they thrust him out of that place. Indeed he also hurried to get out, because the LORD had struck him. And King Uzziah was **a leper to the day of his death**, and being a **leper** lived in a **separate house**, for he was **excluded** from the house of the LORD* (2Chronicles 26:16–21).

Following his introductory statement concerning Uzziah, Isaiah goes on to describe his vision of God Almighty, seated on his throne with the train of his robe filling the entire temple. Six-winged seraphim flew about in the temple, covering their faces with two of their wings in order not to look upon the awesome majesty that was God Almighty. As they flew the seraphim cried responsively one to another, "*Holy, holy, holy is the Lord of hosts; the whole earth is full of his glory!*"

Isaiah is awestricken. He backs away into the doorway of the temple, but the doorposts themselves are trembling at the voice of him that sat on the throne and the temple itself is filled with smoke, the cloud of the glory of God Almighty. The prophet blurts out: "*Woe is me, for I am undone [ruined]! Because **I am a man of unclean lips, and I dwell in the midst of a people of unclean lips;** for my eyes have seen the King, the* LORD *of hosts.*"

Isaiah was a very holy man, yet he saw himself as a leper; this was in comparison to the majesty and holiness of GodAlmighty that he saw, for that is the reason for Isaiah's unclean lips:

*Anyone with the leprous disease must wear torn clothes, let their hair be disheveled, **cover their mustache and lower lip and cry out,** "Unclean! Unclean!" As long as they have the disease they remain **unclean**. They must **live alone**; they must live **outside** the camp*
(Leviticus 13:45–46).

Leprosy was contagious and lepers dwelt alone outside the camp, as did king Uzziah, he, being a leper, lived in a separate house, for he was excluded from the house of the LORD. Isaiah did not just see himself as a leper in comparison to God Almighty, he saw the whole house of Israel as a community of lepers. And when we, the redeemed of the LORD, care to think back to what we formerly were, and then compare our "non-existent holiness" to the actual holiness of Jesus, the Son of God Almighty, we can appreciate that we, too, were lepers in comparison.

Let us leave the leprosy question for a few moments while we take a brief look at the ceremonial cleansing of the priests of Israel and their anointing. The priests were in a category of their own, and they were consecrated and wholly separated from the people solely to minister to the Lord:

*Then you shall kill the ram, and take some of its blood and put it on the **tip of the right ear** of Aaron and on the **tip of the right ear** of his sons, on the **thumb of their right hand** and on the **big toe of their right foot**, and sprinkle the blood all around on the altar. And you shall take some of the blood that is on the altar, and some of the **anointing oil**, and sprinkle it on Aaron and on his garments, on his sons and on the garments of his sons with him; and **he and his garments shall be hallowed**, and his sons and his sons' garments with him* (Exodus 29:20–21).

*Then Moses took some of the anointing oil and some of the blood which was on the altar, and sprinkled it on Aaron, on his garments, on his sons, and on the garments of his sons with him; and he **consecrated** Aaron, his garments, his sons, and the garments of his sons with him* (Leviticus 8:30). And Moses said: *And you shall not go outside the door of the tabernacle of meeting for seven days, until **the days of your consecration** are ended. For seven days he shall consecrate you. As he has done this day, so the Lord*

has commanded to do, **to make atonement for you**
                                        (Leviticus 8:33–34).

Now let us return again to the leprosy situation. Lepers
were unclean all their days until a priest examined them
and had declared them clean. The former lepers were
then able to enter the Camp of the LORD's people and
begin life anew, and with much joy. There was, however,
a ritual that the leper must first undergo in order to be
pronounced clean by the priest:

*The priest shall take some of the blood of the trespass
offering, and the priest shall put it on the* **tip of the right
ear** *of him who is to be cleansed, on the* **thumb of his
right hand**, *and on the* **big toe of his right foot**. *And the
priest shall take some of the log of oil, and pour it into
the palm of his own left hand. Then the priest shall dip
his right finger in the oil that is in his left hand, and shall
sprinkle some of the oil with his finger seven times before
the Lord. And of the rest of the oil in his hand, the priest
shall put some on the* **tip of the right ear** *of him who is
to be cleansed, on the* **thumb of his right hand**, *and on
the* **big toe of his right foot**, *on the blood of the trespass
offering. The rest of the oil that is in the priest's hand he
shall put* **on the head** *of him who is* **to be cleansed**. *So the
priest shall* **make atonement for him** *before the* LORD.

*Then the priest shall offer the sin offering, and
make atonement for him who is to be cleansed from his
uncleanness. Afterward he shall kill the burnt offering.
And the priest shall offer the burnt offering and the grain
offering on the altar. So* **the priest shall make atonement
for him, and he shall be clean** (Leviticus 14:14–20).

As already said: before redemption we were all lepers in comparison to the Lord—*We have **all become like one who is unclean, and all our righteous deeds are like a polluted garment**. We all fade like a leaf, and our iniquities, like the wind, take us away* (Isaiah 64:6).

But lepers can be cleansed in exactly the same way as the priests are cleansed, sanctified, and anointed; and every truly twice-born Christian helps constitute the **kingdom of priests to our God**. The blood that **Jesus our high priest** puts on our leprous **right ears, right thumbs and right big toe is his blood,** the atoning blood of God's *only begotten Son,* sacrificially shed for us at Calvary, and **the oil is the anointing oil of the Holy Spirit**. The blood put on the ears symbolizes the blood daubed on the lintels of the houses of God's people in Egypt, and that on the thumbs and toes that of the door posts. It is the application of the blood of Jesus—God Almighty's *Passover Lamb*—to our ears, thumbs and toes that will avert death for us on the great and terrible *day of vengeance, the Day of God Almighty.*

And what applied to God's people Israel, applies even more so to the redeemed, to those who have been **washed in the blood** (Revelation 1:5) of God Almighty's sacrificial lamb: *And you shall be to me **a kingdom of priests** and **a holy nation*** (Exodus 19:6).

*You are a chosen generation, **a royal priesthood, a holy nation**, his own special people, that you may proclaim the praises of him who called you out of darkness into his marvelous light* (1Peter 2:9).

Every leper and every defiled person was separated from the body of Israel and lived apart, outside of the camp of the Lord:

*And the Lord spoke to Moses, saying: "Command the children of Israel that they put out of the camp every leper, everyone who has a discharge, and whoever becomes defiled by a corpse. You shall **put out both male and female; you shall put them outside the camp, that they may not defile their camps in the midst of which I dwell"***
(Numbers 5:1–3).

Should we not also strictly apply this principle to the Church? Should not the redeemed of the LORD put out of the Church all the modern-day "*lepers*"—everyone who is "*unclean*"—those who **practice** hypocrisy and whoever becomes **defiled** by the **practice** of sin. We should put out both the male and female spiritual fraudsters; we should put them **outside** the Church, that they may **not defile the churches in the midst of which Jesus walks**. Unfortunately, the Church also has more than its share of professional charlatans—corrupt leaders and members who live high from their shadowy pickings taken from the naive, and from widows and orphans, those who *run greedily in the error of Balaam for profit* (Jude 11). They need to be banished from the camp, they are *unclean*, they defile the Church. The lepers who live outside the camp (Church) should be welcomed with open arms and shown the way of cleansing and salvation, but the lepers who dwell within the Camp (Church) should be excommunicated for as long as it takes them to come into full repentance.

The Lord Jesus Christ desires an undefiled Church, a spotless, holy Church washed in his blood and in the water of God's word:

*Husbands, **love** your wives, just as **Christ also loved the church and gave himself for her**, that he might **sanctify** and **cleanse** her with the **washing** of water by the **word**, that he might present her to himself a **glorious church, not having spot or wrinkle or any such thing, but that she should be holy and without blemish***

(Ephesians 5:25–27).

We are a **kingdom of priests** to our God. Priests were and still are a separate class and relationship with God shows itself in separation. The true Christian feels no more at home in this world than the Patriarch Abraham did when he set out from Ur of the Chaldees for the land of Canaan. If he spoke the language he spoke it with an accent—he was called Abraham the Hebrew (Genesis 14:13)—they all knew he was not one of them. Personal relationship with God in the Old Testament showed itself in separation, and this is symbolized by Abraham's separation from his country and from his kith and kin. Abraham's very faith separated him from those around him; our calling as priests to our God should naturally and spiritually separate us from the world. Just as Abraham had no inheritance in the land of Canaan, we have no inheritance in this earthly world. Our inheritance is divine—God Almighty is *our inheritance*, he is *our possession*:

*It shall be, in regard to their inheritance, that **I am their inheritance**. You shall give them no possession in Israel, for **I am their possession*** (Ezekiel 44:28).

As priests in God's kingdom our *inheritance* is God himself; he is our *possession*! Our lips have been cleansed by coals taken from the altar and our *iniquities* have been *taken away, and our sin purged* with the atoning blood of Jesus Christ; we are no longer lepers and a people of unclean lips, we are now *a cleansed kingdom of priests*.

It is not possible to truly understand the New Testament without first understanding the Old Testament: the New is concealed in the Old, and the Old is revealed in the New.

Dear Lord:
Help us to understand that whatever is found in the New Testament can be traced back to the Old Testament. Please help us not to just accept things we hear or read, but to **search the Scriptures daily** *to see if these things are so* (Acts 17:11). Help us to **Study** *to show ourselves approved by God, workmen that need not be ashamed, rightly handling the word of truth* (2Timothy 2:15). Help us to truly understand what it means to be a priest in the kingdom of God, and that you indeed are our *inheritance*; that you are our *possession*. Cause us to seek to know you more. Make us hungry and thirsty for the knowledge of you. Amen.

Blessing and Cursing

I have covered this issue in another book; however, it is such an important topic for Christian debate because it provides the key to many a person's lack of progress in their spiritual walk with Jesus. In Genesis 12:1-3 there is a particular passage that is mostly quoted by Christians in reference to the worldwide Christian community; however, the Scripture is literally directed toward the patriarch Abraham and his physical descendants through his son Isaac, namely the Jews. There is great misunderstanding concerning this passage and that misunderstanding will remain with us as long as the translators of major English-language versions of the Bible continue to follow "traditional" renderings rather than stepping out of their Christian comfort zones and become faithful in accurately translating the text.

Most, but not all English versions, render the passage the same as the *New King James* version given below. The portion in question is emphasized and quoted in context with its two preceding verses.

Now the LORD had said to Abram: "Get out of your country, from your family and from your father's house, to a land that I will show you. I will make you a great nation; I will bless you and make your name great; and you shall be a blessing. **I will bless those who bless you, and I will curse him who curses you;** *and in you all the families of the earth shall be blessed"* (Genesis 12:1-3).

God Almighty is telling Abram, the grandfather of Jacob, whom he later renamed Israel, that he would become a *"great nation."* Today, that nation could be Israel, which has a populaton of some eight million people and is a world leader in many areas. It could also refer to the *Israel of God* (Galatians 6:16), which has hundreds of millions of citizens who, like Abraham, are God-fearing.

However, the LORD continues by saying that he would make Abraham's name *"great; and **you shall be a blessing** ... in you **all the families of the earth shall be blessed**."* This promise would apply equally to both physical Israel and also to the *Israel of God.*

Abraham is known as the father of faith, because he *believed God and it was counted to him as righteousness* (Galatians 3:6), and God called him *"**My friend**"* (Isaiah 41:8). And all those of like faith *are the **sons** of Abraham* (Galatians 3:7), and Jesus says they are *"**My friends**"* (John 15:14).

However, God's promises to Abraham were to come through Abraham's son Isaac, *the son of promise* (Galatians 4:28), with whom God *established his covenant and with his descendents after him* (Genesis 17:19). Abraham's direct physical descendents coming through Isaac are the Jewish people.

I need not spend much time on the the greatness of the Jewish people, nor on the aspect of the blessing that they have been to all the nations of the earth. They are a unique and wonderful people—creative and talented, with a passion for life and culture. The contribution the Jews have made to the world is enormous. They comprise only a small fraction of one percent of the world's population, yet they have produced more than ten percent of the world's Nobel Prize winners.

The genius of the Jews in the fields of Science, Medicine, and the Arts is legendary. And through the Jewish people came the Bible and Jesus, *the Lamb of God who takes away the sin of the world* (John 1:29). Of course we know that Jesus was and is *the Son of God*, but Jesus came into this world of men as a Jew and he lived as a Jew, and there is the sure words of Scripture: **Jesus Christ is the same yesterday, today, and forever** (Hebrews13:8), and **salvation is from the Jews** (John 4:22).

Therefore, Jesus was and is a Jew. Focusing only upon Jesus, putting aside everything else the Jewish people have contributed to our world, we are told that the Gentiles (non-Jews) were:

strangers from the covenants of promise, **having no hope and without God** *in the world* (Ephesians 2:12).

Without the Jews there would be no Jesus, and without Jesus there would be no **hope**, no **salvation**, and no **God** of love for the non-Jew. Gentiles owe a huge debt to the Jewish people.

Returning to our initial passage in Genesis 12:1–3, I will now isolate the portion where the aforementioned misunderstanding lies, and in parenthesis I place the Hebrew words used (Hebrew is read from right to left):

I will **bless** (ברוך) *those who bless* (ברוך) *you*, and I will **curse** (ארר) *him who curses* (קלל) *you* (Genesis 12:3).

Both the blessing and the cursing is dependent upon a person's attitude toward Abraham and his physical descendants through his son Isaac, who are the Jews.

What is done to them is the same as doing it to the LORD, thus we find written God's words concerning the Jewish people: *He who harms you sticks his finger in my eye!* (Zechariah 2:8).

To "*bless*" (ברוך) means "to honor or to bestow favor upon" and God Almighty promises to do this to all those who honor and favor the Jewish people. However, the next segment, "*I will curse him who curses you*," misleads us by being wrongly translated. At first glance (at least in the popular English-language versions), it would seem to be a divine tit-for-tat statement, but in Hebrew it is not at all moderate.

    First of all, the two words translated here as "*curse*" are quite different in Hebrew (see above). Second of all, they are not only different, but actually poles apart in meaning and do not even come from the same root. The first Hebrew word translated "*curse*" is ארר (*arar*) and the second is קלל (*kilel*). Even without knowledge of Hebrew the reader can readily see that these words have no similarity. There are only two instances in the entire Bible where these two words come together in a single verse, namely, the one that we are giving attention to and the following:

*You shall not **revile** (קלל) God, nor **curse** (ארר) a ruler of your people* (Exodus 22:28).

Here the word קלל (**kilel**) is translated as "**revile**." It is exactly the same Hebrew word used in the verse in Genesis, but translated quite differently. Now let me proceed and analyze what this means to us in real terms.

    We should remember that it is the LORD God Almighty who is speaking these words. It is the LORD who will "*bless*," and it is the LORD who will "*curse*." God Almighty's powerful blessings cause us to rejoice:

*The **blessing** of the LORD makes one rich, and he adds no sorrow with it* (Proverbs 10:22).

*I will ... open for you the windows of heaven and pour out for you **such blessing** that there will not be room enough to receive it* (Malachi 3:10).

Conversely, the LORD's judgments and power are found in his curses:

*So the LORD God said to the serpent: "Because you have done this, you are **cursed** more than all cattle, and more than every beast of the field; **on your belly you shall go**, and you shall eat dust all the days of your life"*
(Genesis 3:14).

That serpent, or snake, once walked upon this earth like the four-legged animals. Most people are unaware that snakes have atrophied legs tucked up inside their bodies—a perpetual, living reminder to the dreadful power of God's curse.

*Then to Adam He said, "Because you have heeded the voice of your wife, and have eaten from the tree of which I commanded you, saying, You shall not eat of it: Cursed is the ground for your sake; **in toil you shall eat of it all the days of your life**. Both **thorns and thistles it shall bring forth** for you, and you shall eat the herb of the field"*
(Genesis 3:17-18).

Adam originally ate food that was self-perpetuated from the soil. After the LORD cursed the ground, mankind sweated and still sweats to extract food from the earth.

The several hundred varieties of thistles that wage war against farmers and gardeners substantiate the curse upon the earth, as do the thousands of dreadful thorn and briar bushes that tear both skin and clothing.

We see the tragic results of the curse of the LORD concerning Jericho (uttered from the lips of Joshua but, nevertheless, the word of the LORD):

*Cursed be the man before the LORD who rises up and builds this city Jericho; he shall lay **its foundation with his firstborn**, and **with his youngest he shall set up its gates** (Joshua 6:26).*

And later we read:

*In his days Hiel of Bethel built Jericho. He laid its foundation **with Abiram his firstborn**, and **with his youngest son Segub he set up its gates**, according to the word of the LORD, which He had spoken through Joshua the son of Nun (1Kings 16:34).*

Hiel thought to rebuild Jericho and his oldest son, his firstborn son, died as he laid the foundations. When he hung the gates to the city his youngest son died also.

In all three of the passages cited above (there are a number of others) the word rendered "*curse*" is, in the original Hebrew, the word ארר (*arar*). The word means: "to execrate," or "to denounce evil against"—"something that brings great harm or trouble." In contrast to this terrible word, we look at the second Hebrew word קלל (*kilel*). I have emphasized the word in its context and have used several English-language versions of the Bible so that we may clearly see its meaning:

When she saw that she had conceived, her mistress became **despised** *in her eyes* (Genesis 16:4 *NKJV*).

You shall not **revile** *God, nor curse a ruler of your people* (Exodus 22:28 *NKJV*).

Do not **blaspheme** *God or curse the ruler of your people* (Exodus 22:28 *NIV*).

Forty blows he may give him and no more, lest he should exceed this and beat him with many blows above these, and your brother be **humiliated** *in your sight* (Deuteronomy 25:3 *NKJV*).

They went into the temple of their god, ate and drank, and **ridiculed** *Abimelech* (Judges 9:27 *NRSV*).

I am **unworthy**—*how can I reply to you?* (Job 40:4 *NIV*).

The LORD *of hosts has purposed ... to bring into* **contempt** *all the honorable of the earth* (Isaiah 23:9 *NKJV*).

We have here six passages with seven different translations of the same word from three major English-language versions of the Bible published in the United States. The following definitions are taken from *Webster's Unabridged Dictionary* published in the United States:

Despise: "to look down upon, to have a low opinion of."

Revile: "to be reproachful or abusive in speech."

Blaspheme: "to revile or speak reproachfully."

Humiliate: "to lower the pride or dignity of; to humble."

Ridicule: "words or actions intended to express contempt and excite laughter."

Unworthy: "without merit or value."

Contempt: "the feeling or actions of a person toward something he considers low, worthless, or beneath notice."

With these definitions in hand we have a much clearer understanding of what is really being said in Genesis 12:3.

The LORD God Almighty has promised to *curse*; to bring great trouble and harm to those who have a low opinion of the Jewish people.

The LORD promises to *curse* and bring great trouble upon those who cause the dignity or the personal pride of the Jewish people to suffer.

The LORD promises to *curse* and bring great trouble upon those who subject the Jewish people to ridicule.

The LORD promises to *curse* and bring great trouble upon those who reproach the Jewish people or subject them to abusive language.

The LORD promises to *curse* and bring great trouble upon those who think that the Jew is lacking in worth or that an individual Jew, or the Jewish people as a whole, are inferior or beneath notice.

The LORD promises to *curse* and bring great trouble upon those that speak reproachfully of his chosen people.

Just as the LORD, through Joshua, issued a warning concerning Jericho, so he also issues a warning to the world at large regarding the Jews.

At the very beginning, when Abram, the father of the Jewish people, stood alone and without offspring, the LORD identifies the cause of Abram with his own. He declares him to be essentially connected with the prosperity and the misfortune of all who come in contact with him. The LORD promises to **bless** those that **bless** Abram and his offspring and, conversely, promises to *curse* those who hold them lightly in esteem. He issued the promises more than 4,000 years ago and the passing of the eons of time has not diluted the blessing nor worn away the severity of the curse. *He who has ears to hear, let him hear.* What the LORD said to Abram still stands today and many people are skating on extremely thin ice with regard to being cursed. In addition to the world's unregenerate population, there are countless numbers of professing Christians who have testimonies of troubled lives; all they touch turns to dust. It behooves us to heed the warning of the LORD concerning the nation of Israel and the Jewish people as a whole. And in blessing, we shall surely be blessed.

Dear Lord,
Forgive me for my wrong understanding of your words. Forgive me, too, the times that I have spoken against your chosen people. Forgive me for the Jewish jokes I laughed at; for holding Jews lightly in esteem. I repent, LORD, and ask that you put my sin under the blood of Jesus, the King of the Jews. Grant me the grace to bless your people in deed and in word and put right the wrongs committed. I now understand that I cannot love the King of the Jews and have a shadow of anti-Semitism in my heart. Amen.

A Virgin shall Conceive

There has been a contention long-held by some, mainly by Jews, that Mary did not fit the divine requirement of her being a true virgin, able to fulfill the prophecy of Isaiah:

*Therefore the Lord himself will give you a sign: behold, **the virgin shall conceive and bear a Son**, and shall call his name **Immanuel**, which is translated, "God with us"*
(Isaiah 7:14).

The contention arises because the Hebrew word used for virgin in the prophecy is עלמה (*alma*), but Mary was a בתולה (*betulah*). The argument against Mary being a virgin because she was not an עלמה (*alma*) is a pointless one and does not hold water, it merely shows the person's lack of Bible knowledge and biblical culture.

If we go to the story of Abraham's chief servant who sought, at Abraham's instruction, a virgin wife for his son Isaac, from Abraham's own people in Mesopotamia. We read that the servant (probably Eliezer of Damascus – Genesis 15:2) arrived at the city of Nahor and waited by the well at the time the women and girls come for water. He made his camels kneel down by the well and prayed that God would bring success for his master by showing him which maiden was to be the bride for Isaac. The servant prayed:

Behold, here I stand by the well of water, and the daughters of the men of the city are coming out to draw water. Now let it be that the young woman to whom I say, "Please

*let down your pitcher that I may drink," and she says,
"Drink, and I will also give your camels a drink"—let her
be the one you have appointed for your servant Isaac. And
by this I will know that you have shown kindness to my
master* (Genesis 24:13–14).

And before the servant had finished praying, Rebecca,
Abraham's niece, came to the well with a pitcher for
water:

Now the young woman was very beautiful to behold, a
virgin (בתולה); *no man had known her. And she went
down to the well, filled her pitcher, and came up. And the
servant ran to meet her and said, "Please let me drink
a little water from your pitcher." So she said, "Drink, my
lord." Then she quickly let her pitcher down to her hand,
and gave him a drink. And when she had finished giving
him a drink, she said, "I will draw water for your camels
also, until they have finished drinking." Then she quickly
emptied her pitcher into the trough, ran back to the well
to draw water, and drew for all his camels. And the man,
wondering at her, remained silent so as to know whether
the Lord had made his journey prosperous or not.*

*So it was, when the camels had finished drinking,
that* **the man took a golden nose ring weighing half a
shekel, and two bracelets for her wrists weighing ten
shekels of gold** (Genesis 24:16–22).

Abraham's servant put the nose ring on Rebecca's nose
and the bracelets on her wrists; and this constituted an
engagement. The servant then asked Rebecca whose
daughter she was and if there were room for him to
lodge at her father's house, to which Rebecca answered

that there was plenty of room for him at the house and also straw and feed for his camels. Rebecca then ran to tell her mother's household everything that had just taken place.

Rebecca had a brother named Laban. When Laban saw the nose ring and the bracelets on his sister's wrists, and had heard her words telling all of what Abraham's servant had spoken to her, he went out to greet the servant and said to him: *"Come in, O blessed of the LORD! Why do you stand outside?"* (Genesis 24:31).

However, Abraham's servant refused to eat until he had told the purpose for his journey from Canaan. He recounted his prayer to them, virtually word for word:

*Behold, I stand by the well of water; and it shall come to pass that when the **virgin** comes out to draw water, and I say to her, "Please give me a little water from your pitcher to drink," and she says to me, "Drink, and I will draw for your camels also,"—let her be the woman whom the Lord has appointed for my master's son* (Genesis 24:43–44).

The difference here is that the Hebrew word used now for "virgin" is no longer בתולה (*betulah*), but עלמה (*alma*), because Rebecca was now betrothed to Isaac, just as Mary was betrothed to Joseph when she bore Jesus. As stated above, the contention that Mary, the mother of Jesus, was not an עלמה (*alma*)—Greek παρθένον (*parthenos*)—and therefore did not fulfill Isaiah's prophecy, simply does not hold water.

Besides those who contend about Mary's purity, there are thousands of "Christians" and others who do not believe in the virgin birth; they say that such a thing is impossible. Some Bible translations reinforce this ungodly, unbelieving line of thought by simply leaving out the fact that it is a virgin that will conceive. Following are three of these versions:

New Revised Standard Version: *Therefore the* LORD *himself will give you a sign. Look,* **the young woman is with child** *and shall bear a son* (Isaiah 7:14).

The NET Bible: *For this reason the sovereign master himself will give you a confirming sign. Look,* **this young woman is about to conceive** *and will give birth to a son* (Isaiah 7:14).

The Bible in Basic English: *For this cause the* LORD *himself will give you a sign;* **a young woman is now with child**, *and she will give birth to a son* (Isaiah 7:14).

Then there is at least one version that skirts the issue with its confusing translation that leaves the reader with doubt about an actual virgin birth:

The Message: *So the Master is going to give you a sign anyway. Watch for this:* **A girl who is presently a virgin will get pregnant** (Isaiah 7:14).

It is difficult to understand those who deny the virgin birth. Isaiah says that ***God will give a sign***. God Almighty is the source of this sign that had been prophesied by Isaiah. It is God himself who gave it. What is extraordinary about a young woman conceiving and bearing a child? All around the world millions do that every day and have done for thousands of years. Obviously, this sign will be an extraordinary phenomenon, nothing short of miraculous: *a virgin shall conceive*. Now that is a miraculous sign given by a God with whom *nothing is too difficult* (Jeremiah 32:17), *who gives life to the dead and **calls those things which do not exist as though they did*** (Romans 4:17). Substituting young woman in place of virgin shows the spiritual bankruptcy of the translator and editor alike.

I have a cup at home that I bought in a Chinese peasant market in a village in the middle of China in 1988. It is a large cup, bigger than a coffee mug, and is covered in a myriad of hand-painted flowers on a black glazing. It quickly became my favorite cup and I used it every day for years, until I tripped on some stone stairs as I took it up to my office. I endeavored to protect the cup as I fell, but it smacked down hard on the stonework and was badly damaged. A jagged crack went almost from the top to the bottom of the cup and the glazing and flowers around the crack were badly chipped. I was very upset because I had become attached to the cup. My wife looked at it and said consolingly, "It could last for years like that," but it did not console me.

The cup did not leak so I continued to use it, but the magic had gone. One day, as I rinsed the cup after coming down from my office, I noticed the crack had disappeared. I got a magnifying glass and examined the cup carefully; there was no crack and there was no chipped glazing or chipped flowers. I called my wife into the kitchen and said, "God has healed my cup!" She took the cup, turned it around and around, and said, incredulously, "How did he do that!" The cup is now in pride of place in our glass-doored china cabinet. The point in me telling this story is because God can do anything. At no time did I ask God to mend my broken cup; he did it on his own volition because he loves me, just as he does everyone else in his family. And if God can mend a broken cup so perfectly that the use of a magnifying glass cannot detect where the break had been, he can equally as effortlessly and undetectably implant his holy seed into a virgin's womb without her knowing the actual date she became pregnant by that miraculous act of God Almighty. Mary was a virgin; she was a sign from God. Accept it!

Dear Lord,
I thank you that you provided mankind with a sign, a phenomenally miraculous sign—that of a virgin giving birth. And this was fulfilled by Mary who gave birth to Jesus in a stable in Bethlehem. Help us Lord to completely shed any doubts we may have about your great love, your immense power, and your ability to keep your promises. Help us to be *fully convinced that what God had promised, God is also able to perform* (Romans 4:21 Paraphrased). Amen.

Angry? No, Only Upset

There is a familiar scripture passage that most of us read and end up feeling empathy for king David. The king was doing his level best to bring the Ark of the Covenant back to Jerusalem; however, there was a prescribed ritual concerning the Ark, but it was not being followed. David had the Ark placed on a new cart to be transported to Jerusalem (the Ark should have been carried on the shoulders of the Levites, not placed on a cart. David got this right the second time around—2Samuel 6:10–15), but the Lord struck Uzza, one of the drivers of the cart, because when the oxen stumbled he put his hand out onto the Ark to steady it.

*Then **the anger** of the Lord was aroused against Uzza, and he struck him because he put his hand to the ark; and he died there before God. And David became **angry** because of the Lord's outbreak against Uzza; therefore that place is called Perez Uzza to this day. David **was afraid of God that day**, saying, "How can I bring the ark of God to me?"* (1Chronicles 13:10–12).

Following the death of Uzza David became afraid of God Almighty, and the Ark was left with Obed-Edom for three months until David figured out what went wrong. Virtually all English-language translations have David becoming "*angry*" with God over Uzza being struck dead, but this was really not the case. In both Hebrew and Arabic the nose can indicate both anger and the sign of a sickness. The face of a person who gets really angry turns a shade of red from increased blood pressure, and this includes the nose. And when a person contracts influenza or some other virus, where mucus must exit via the nasal passages, the person's nose can become quite red. The latter person, especially in Arab culture, will say that he is "upset," not feeling well.

In our passage of scripture we have the anger of the LORD being aroused against Uzza because he touched the holy Ark, and the LORD's anger is expressed thus (reading from right to left): ויחר-אף יהוה, which tells us that the LORD's nose was hot. On the other hand, David is said to be angry, but his anger is rendered: ויחר, which means he was not angry, but *hot, burning*; in other words David was "upset" at Uzza's sudden death and wondered how on earth he was ever going to get the Ark back to the City of David. Looking at the Hebrew text, we read in the first three words on the first line, "*And the **anger** of the LORD...*," and on the second line, the first two words, "*And David **burned**....*" David was understandingly upset at the LORD's outbreak again Uzza, but, as mentioned earlier, David rectified his mistake three months later. Below is the full Hebrew text:

ויכהו על אשר-שלח ידו על-הארון וימת שם לפני אלהים
ויחר-אף יהוה בעזא
פרץ בעזא ויקרא למקום ההוא פרץ עזא עד היום הזה
ויחר לדויד כי-פרץ יהוה
ביום ההוא לאמר היך אביא אלי את ארון האלהים
ויירא דויד את-האלהים

(1Chronicles 13:10–12)

Translators certainly missed this one. Following a little research it seems to me that only the *Literal Translation of the Bible* by Jay P. Green has the correct translation of David being "*upset*" and not "*angry*."

There are many scripture passages that brings the "nose" (אַף) into prominent focus concerning anger. For example, we are told that: *An angry man stirs up strife* (Proverbs 29:22). In Hebrew that "*angry man*" is אַף-אִישׁ, which literally means "nose man" and here we see the "nose" (אַף) prominently featured. Similarly we are told: *Make no friendship with an **angry man*** (Proverbs 22:24). This time the Hebrew used is בַּעַל אַף, which really means "lord" or "master" "of the nose." But just as king David was upset and not angry, there are passages equally as misleading:

*Be **angry**, and do not sin. Meditate within your heart on your bed, and be still* (Psalms 4:4). Here the word translated "angry" is רִגְזוּ (*rigzu*), which does not mean angry at all, but "exited," "tremble," or "disturbed." It is good to see that the *New International Version* translates the verse correctly:

***Tremble** and do not sin; when you are on your beds, search your hearts and be silent* (Psalms 4:4 *NIV*). And the *New Revised Standard Version* also has it: *When you are **disturbed**, do not sin; ponder it on your beds, and be silent* (Psalms 4:4 *NRSV*).

In conclusion, let me say that Bible translation is a difficult task, especially if translators are not intimately familiar with the cultures of the Bible, so there are bound to be inaccuracies. We can all but do our best.

Dear Lord:

Thank you for your indestructible, incorruptible word that has been handed down for thousands of years, and which has gone out into the four corners of the world, bringing salvation and hope to countless millions. Thank you for every translator that has labored over your word, interpreting it into hundreds of languages. We understand that no translation is perfect, but help us as individuals to use the many tools available that will help shed light on difficult passages. Help each one of us to: *Study to show ourselves approved before God, workmen that need not to be ashamed, rightly handling the word of truth* (2Timothy 2:15). Amen.

Doorkeepers

Psalms 84:10 says: *For a day in your courts is better than a thousand elsewhere. I would rather be a doorkeeper in the house of my God than dwell in the tents of wickedness.*

Only atheists and evildoers would not agree with that! Some Christians will, with complete spontaneity, only quote just the best-known portion of the psalm: *I would rather be a doorkeeper in the house of the Lord than dwell in the tents of wickedness.* Again, only atheists and evildoers would not agree. However, probably the majority of those quoting this passage misunderstand what it really says. Most English-language versions have missed its meaning by following tradition and therefore lead their readers down the wrong path.

King David, *the sweet psalmist of Israel* (2Samuel 23:1) supposedly wrote Psalm 84. I say "supposedly" because some of the psalms that carry David's name were not written by him, but by others who put David's name to them, therefore I shall just refer to "the writer." Whoever wrote this psalm, that writer expressed his heart's longing for God Almighty. The office of doorkeeper in the house of God was a coveted position and one of trust. And whereas the population of Israel was numbered in the millions, only two hundred men were appointed as doorkeepers by King David:

All those chosen as gatekeepers were two hundred and twelve. They were recorded by their genealogy, in their villages. **David and Samuel the seer** *had appointed them to their* **trusted office.** *So they and their children were in charge of the gates of the house of the Lord, the house of the tabernacle, by assignment. The gatekeepers were assigned to the four directions: the east, west, north, and south. And their brethren in their villages had to come with them from time to time for seven days. For* **in this trusted office were four chief gatekeepers; they were Levites. And they had charge over the chambers and treasuries of the house of God. And they lodged all around the house of God because they had the responsibility,** *and they were in charge of opening it every morning*

(1Chronicles 9:22–27).

None but the priests were allowed to enter into the inner and innermost courts of the house of God, not even the king. Longing to enter the inner courts, but religiously barred from entry, the writer expresses his thoughts that just one day in those courts would be better than a thousand days elsewhere. He is saying that he would choose to humble himself and just sit by the door-post, on the threshold, like a beggar, for that would be preferable to living outside among the unrighteous.

The Hebrew word סָפַף (*safaf*), which is translated "*doorkeeper*," is only found this one time in the Bible, it comes from the noun סַף (saf), which means "threshold." The *New American Standard* at least furnishes the correct sense of the writer's heart:

For a day in Your courts is better than a thousand outside. I would rather stand at **the threshold** *of the house of my God than dwell in the tents of wickedness*

(Psalms 84:10 *NASB*).

The *NET* version appears to gets close:

Certainly spending just one day in your **temple** *courts is better than spending a thousand elsewhere. I would rather stand at* **the entrance** *to the* **temple** *of my God than live in the tents of the wicked* (Psalms 84:10 *NET*).

I said the above version "appears" to get close to the real meaning; there was no *temple* in King David's day, that came later by the hand of his son Solomon years after David's death, which also adds credence to the opinion that this and some other psalms not having been written by David:

Go and tell my servant David, "Thus says the LORD*: 'Would you build a* **house** *for me to dwell in? For* **I have not dwelt in a house since the time that I brought the children of Israel up from Egypt, even to this day, but have moved about in a tent and in a tabernacle'"* (2Samuel 7:5–6).

The Hebrew word in Psalm 84 that the *NET* version translated as "*temple*" is בית (*beit*), meaning "house," which is often used in the Old Testament to portray the *house of God*, and is the word used by the LORD himself when he says to David, "*Would you build a* **house** *for me"?*

The Hebrew word for "temple" is היכל (*hechal*) and is used ten times in the Psalms. The Hebrew word for "house" is בית (*beit*) and is used twenty-two times in the Psalms refering to the *house of God*. It is a complete mystery to me why the *NET* version would substitute "*temple*" when the Hebrew text so clearly says "*house*."

I do not wish to be unkind, but putting "*temple*" in this instance instead of "*house*" is a little like all the maps at the back of a zillion Bibles that show **"Palestine in the time of Christ"** when there was no such entity in existence at that time, nor had there ever been. Jesus was born in Bethlehem, in *Israel*; he lived in Nazareth, an *Israeli* city; he was crucified and resurrected in *Jerusalem*, the main city and spiritual center of *Israel*.

All these blunders are made by experts and lead readers down a wrong path, but, as Abba Eban said, "An expert is one who knows everything, but nothing else."

I went off on a tangent about "house" versus "temple" because I believe that substituting one for another is being unfaithful to the word of God and is misleading for Bible students. As stated previously, "house" is often a synonym for the *house of God*, but sometimes there is a differentiation that cannot be put down to the penchant by writers of the Hebrew Scriptures to use parallel construction. For example:

But as for me, because of your great faithfulness I will **enter your house**; *I will* **bow down toward your holy temple** *as I worship you* (Psalms 5:7).

If the writer of this psalm enters the "*house*" (*house of God*), how is it possible for him to bow down *toward* it when he is already in it? I believe this tells us something we have not heretofore paid attention to. I am of the opinion that "*house*," when used of the *house of God*, means the entire structure together with all its courts and substructures. I believe the "*temple*," on the other hand, specifically refers to the "*Holy of Holies*," the *sanctum sanctorum* of holy places, the place where God dwells. In Hebrew it is called the קדוש הקדשים (*kodesh kodeshim*), it is the most holy place where no man dare set foot except the high priest, and then only once each year on *the Day of Atonement* (Leviticus 23:27). There the LORD of all the earth dwelt; above the *Mercy Seat* made of pure gold that was placed on the *Ark of the Covenant*. The LORD's presence was flanked by two *cherubim* of pure gold who faced each other and whose wings reached across the Ark, across the *Mercy Seat*, and touched one another.

the ark of God, which is called by the Name, the name of the LORD Almighty, **who sits enthroned between the cherubim above the ark** (2Samuel 6:2).

There God dwelt, between the *cherubim*, above the *Mercy Seat*; it was his private, most holy sanctum; his temple. And thus worshipers would enter the "*courts*" of the "*house*" and "*bow down toward the temple*"—toward the *Holy of Holies* where God's presence was.

Dear Lord:
Again we ask for your help in rightly handling your incorruptible, indestructible word. Again we ask that you help us to **study** the many Bible helps that are readily available in the Western world, that would increase our knowledge of the Bible, which is our road-map to knowing more about you; and **the knowledge of the Holy One is insight** (Proverbs 9:10).

Mary of Magdala

A short while ago I read a piece written by a pastor of note in *The Word for you Today*, that Mary Magdalene was a prostitute. Was this really so, or did the pastor do a terrible disservice to the name and memory of Mary Magdalene? Mary loved Jesus with such passion that he revealed himself to her first (Mark 16:9), which was very soon after his resurrection (John 20:14–17). Looking at the scripture verses I think it most likely that there were two different women in the gospels who anointed Jesus with ointment.

The writers of the gospels wrote for different audiences, at different times, and from memory—there were no gadgets or smartphones for recording the life and times of Jesus in their day. Matthew was a little like a modern "hell, fire and brimstone" preacher, he was a Jew who wrote what was relevant for a Jewish audience. Mark wrote for a mixed audience, as did Luke, but Luke gives us far more content, much like a historian. John writes to a mixed audience, but focuses on having his readers believe that Jesus was truly *the Son of God* and John's gospel is mostly different to the other three.

Following are the salient Scriptures regarding the woman (or women) from each of the four gospels in the New Testament gospel order:

*When Jesus was **in Bethany** at the house of **Simon the leper**, a woman came to him having an alabaster flask of* *very costly fragrant oil, and she **poured it on his head** as he sat at the table. But when his disciples saw it, they were indignant, saying, "Why this waste? For this fragrant oil might have been sold for much and given to the poor."*

*But when Jesus was aware of it, he said to them, "Why do you trouble the woman? For she has done a good work for me. For you have the poor with you always, but me you do not have always. For **in pouring this fragrant oil on my body, she did it for my burial***

(**Matthew** 26:6–12).

Matthew unequivocally states that Jesus was in **Bethany** at the house of **Simon the leper**, when the woman poured the oil **on the head** of Jesus, and that Jesus commended her for her **pre-burial** anointing, of his **body**.

*And being in **Bethany** at the house of **Simon the leper**, as he sat at the table, a woman came having an alabaster flask of **very costly oil of spikenard**. Then she **broke the flask and poured it on his head*** (**Mark** 14:3).

Mark follows Matthew in that Jesus was in **Bethany** at the house of **Simon the leper** and that the very costly spikenard oil was poured **on the head** of Jesus.

*One of the **Pharisees** asked [Jesus] to eat with him. And he went to the **Pharisee's** house, and sat down to eat. And behold, a woman in the city who was a sinner, when she knew that Jesus sat at the table in the **Pharisee's** house, brought an alabaster flask of **fragrant oil**, and **stood at his feet behind Him weeping; and she began to wash his feet with her tears**, and wiped them with the hair of her head; and she kissed his feet and anointed them with the* *fragrant oil. Now when the **Pharisee** who had invited him saw this, he spoke to himself, saying, "This man, if he were a prophet, would know who and what manner of woman this is who is touching him, for she is a sinner."*

*And Jesus answered and said to him, "**Simon**, I have something to say to you..." (Luke 7:36–40). ... Then he turned to the woman and said to **Simon**, "Do you see this woman? I entered your house; you gave me no water for my feet, but she has washed my feet with her tears and wiped them with the hair of her head. You gave me no kiss, but this woman has not ceased to kiss my feet since the time I came in. **You did not anoint my head with oil**, but this woman **has anointed My feet** with fragrant oil"*
(**Luke** 7:44–46).

Luke does not denote in which town the act took place, but it was at a house of a **Pharisee** named **Simon**, and it was apparently in the earlier part of Jesus' ministry because Luke was rather chronological in his writings: *"having followed everything from the very beginning"* (Luke 1:3). It is therefore highly unlikely that Luke, an intelligent physician, would be confused over whether it took place in the house of *a Pharisee* named *Simon*, or in the house of *a leper* named *Simon*. It is also highly unlikely that the Pharisee would be a leper because he would be religiously unclean and would have had to have kept his distance.

Luke's woman also *stood behind Jesus, at his feet* (the custom was that people ate reclined on cushions on the floor with the feet stretched out from the table) *weeping*. This woman wept so much that her *tears* fell onto the feet of Jesus and she *wiped them away with her hair* (long hair on a woman was also the custom). Having wiped the feet of Jesus with her hair she then began to *kiss* them and then *anoint* them with "*fragrant oil*," but "*very costly oil of spikenard*" is not mentioned by Luke, only *fragrant oil*. The woman was a "*sinner*," very likely a known prostitute, and had entered the Pharisee's house when she knew Jesus was at the table to eat, she was not an invited guest. Jesus specifically mentions that, only his *feet* were anointed; his *head was not*.

Then, six days before the Passover, Jesus came to Bethany, where Lazarus was who had been dead, whom he had raised from the dead. There they made him a supper; and Martha served, but Lazarus was one of those who sat at the table with him. Then Mary took a pound of very costly oil of spikenard, anointed the feet of Jesus, and wiped his feet with her hair. And the house was filled with the fragrance of the oil.

But one of his disciples, Judas Iscariot, Simon's son, who would betray him, said, "Why was this fragrant oil not sold for three hundred denarii and given to the poor?" This he said, not that he cared for the poor, but because he was a thief, and had the money box; and he used to take what was put in it.

But Jesus said, "Let her alone; she has kept this for the day of my burial" (**John** 12:1–7).

Here John determines for us that it took place *six days before the Passover* meal, after which came the arrest of Jesus and his subsequent crucifixion the following day, so it was at the very end of Jesus' ministry. John corroborates with both Matthew and Mark that the anointing took place in **Bethany**. There they (probably Martha and Mary) made him a supper and **Martha**, as was her wont, **served** (Luke 10:40). Again, the discourse is very different in John's account to that written by Luke.

Then Martha's sister, Mary, **took a pound of very costly oil of spikenard, anointed the feet of Jesus, and wiped his feet with her hair**. In John's account Mary had **a pound**, a very large amount of the **costly oil of spikenard** and must have **anointed** more than just the **feet** of Jesus. Matthew says that a woman (which must refer to Mary) **came to him** (Jesus) and, in contrast to Luke's woman, **poured the oil on his head**; Jesus says it was also **poured on his body**. There is no mention of Mary weeping tears on the feet of Jesus nor kissing them, she purposely anointed his feet with **very costly oil of spikenard and wiped them with her hair**.

Oil poured on the **head**, the **body**, and the **feet** of Jesus would fit the **pound** weight **of spikenard oil** that Mary brought—such a large amount would have been wasted on the anointing of only the *feet*. On the **head**, **body**, and **feet** of Jesus would also fit the anointing **for the day of my burial** as told by Matthew and John. Matthew, Mark, and John testify that it was **very costly oil**, and Mark and John both say it was **oil of spikenard**.

There is little doubt that Matthew, Mark, and John all record the same event in similar, but not identical, words.

We must also take into account the fact that Jesus had **cast seven demons** out of Mary:

Now when he rose early on the first day of the week, he appeared first to **Mary Magdalene, out of whom he had cast seven demons** (**Mark** 16:9).

…and certain women who had been healed of evil spirits and infirmities—Mary called Magdalene, **out of whom had come seven demons** (**Luke** 8:2).

There was no mention of anything with Luke's woman except that Jesus said:

Therefore I say to you [Simon], her sins, **which are many,** *are forgiven, for she loved much. But to whom little is forgiven, the same loves little." Then He said to her, "Your sins are forgiven." And those who sat at the table with Him began to say to themselves, "Who is this who even forgives sins?" Then He said to the woman, "Your faith has saved you. Go in peace"* (**Luke** 7:47–50.

Jesus neither laid hands on this woman, nor commanded spirits to leave. And immediately following the above verse Luke continues with:

Now it came to pass, **afterward,** *that he went through every city and village, preaching and bringing the glad tidings of the kingdom of God. And the twelve were with him, and* **certain women who had been healed of evil spirits** *and infirmities—Mary called Magdalene, out of whom had come seven demons, and Joanna the wife of Chuza, Herod's steward, and Susanna, and many others who* **provided for Him from their substance**

(**Luke** 8:1–3).

How then can the woman who wept on the feet of Jesus be the same woman out of whom **seven demons** had come, whom Luke, in virtually his next breath, identifies as Mary, and who was providing for Jesus along with other women? Surely Luke would have pointed this fact out, much like John did:

*A certain man was sick, Lazarus of Bethany, **the town of Mary and her sister Martha. It was that Mary who anointed the Lord with fragrant oil and wiped His feet with her hair**, whose brother Lazarus was sick*

(John 11:1–2).

John says that it was **Mary who anointed the Lord with fragrant oil and wiped his feet with her hair**, but simply putting fragrant oil on his feet does not constitute **anointing** and John purposely says Mary **anointed** Jesus. And while it may look like John is refering to Luke's woman whose tears fell onto the feet of Jesus and who wiped his feet with her hair; it must be noted that John does not carry that story in his gospel. He is pointing toward the future, not back toward the past. Matthew uses the same type of pointing toward the future when he records the choosing of the twelve apostles by Jesus and references Judas' betrayal far ahead of the deed:

*Simon the Zealot, and **Judas Iscariot, who betrayed him*** (Matthew 10:4).

The idea that Mary was a prostitute and was the woman in Luke's narrative, involving the *Pharisee* named *Simon*, does not, in my opinion, hold water. Luke also records for us:

As they went on their way, Jesus entered a village. And a woman named Martha welcomed him into her house.

And she had a sister called Mary, who sat at the Lord's feet and listened to his teaching. But Martha was distracted with much serving (**Luke** 10:38–40).

Mary must have been freed from her demon possession while being one of the people who made up the great multitudes following and thronging Jesus. Here she now sits at his feet, hanging on his every word. I cannot help but believe there must have been two different women in these stories, one early in Jesus' ministry, and the other at the end of his ministry. I have presented the facts, but you, the reader, must reach your own personal decision based on the scriptural evidence.

Dear Lord:
We know from the different writings in the gospels that the women (or woman) who anointed the feet and body of Jesus loved him very much. We also know that they (or she) were (or was) forgiven their (or her) sins and were (or was) loved and accepted by Jesus in return. Help us to be kind to the memories (or memory) of these women (or this woman). Help us to see only the love that they (or she) had for your *only begotten Son*, and help us to love him in the same extravagantly passionate manner. Amen.

The Memorial Name

The memorial name is the one name by which the LORD commanded men to both know and remember him, but neither Israel nor the Church complies. Israel began with the proper name of God upon its lips, but as man's rules and regulations "fenced-in" the *Torah* (Law), the Biblical religion gave way to the Jewish rabbinical religion that prevails until today. The proper name of God became the "incommunicable" name—the name that was never to be uttered. The Church does not use the proper name of God because the early translators of the Hebrew texts, not knowing about the "fence" the Jewish rabbis had placed around the name, translated it incorrectly.

The rabbis, desiring that no one should ever take God's name in vain (Deuteronomy 5: 11), made a rule that every person was to say "*Adonai*"—(*Lord*), when they read the proper name in the Scriptures or prayer book. They also punctuated the proper name with a system of vowel signs called *nikud*, making the name actually read as if it were "*Lord*." Tradition, both Jewish and Christian (tradition is often as great a curse as it is a blessing), subsequently robbed God of his proper name and the Church of the knowledge of it.

The name to which I refer is used no less than 6,375 times in the Bible and, apart from being translated seven times in the 1611 *King James* version as "*Jehovah*," and as "*Jehovah*" throughout the entire *ASV*, it is translated in every other popular English version as LORD, or

Sovereign Lord (*NIV*). God's personality is revealed in both his Name and his names. We should realize that from the preponderance of the usage alone, this name holds a great deal of importance.

What is translated as "Lord," or "*Jehovah*," are the four Hebrew letters י (*yod*), ה (*heh*), ו (*vav*), ה (*heh*), which constitutes what is commonly known as the Tetragrammaton—the proper name of God. The name has a very distinct meaning, but when the early Bible scholars translated the Hebrew Scriptures into an English version, they followed the rabbinical tradition of using "Lord" as the name of God. Knowing that it was not God's proper name the scholars capitalized it as "Lord" to distinguish it from "Lord"—the equivalent of "Sir." They also attempted to translate the proper name of God, but not realizing that the *nikud* punctuation assigned to the Tetragrammaton by the rabbis was that of "Lord," and not that of the proper name, they translated a totally spurious "Jehovah" in place of "**Yahveh**," the closest pronunciation of God's proper name.

The modem meaning of "Lord" is far from the original meaning, which makes our use of it a mere shadow of its real import. The proper name of God, on the other hand, has lost none of its majestical import. Even though little is found in scholarly works and Bible commentaries on the name, it is not too difficult to comprehend its meaning. The four letters that make up the Tetragrammaton—י (*yod*), ה (*heh*), ו (*vav*), ה (*heh*), are rearranged into three words: ה (*heh*), י (*yod*), ה (*heh*) making היה (*hiyah*), which means "was"); ה (*heh*), ו (*vav*),

ה (*heh*) making הוה (*hoveh*), which means "is"); and י
(*yod*), ה (*heh*), י (*yod*), ה (*heh*) making יהיה (*yihiyeh*),
which means "will be"). The meaning of **Yahveh**, God's
proper name—"*is*," "*was*," "*will be*"—is therefore quite
obvious (at least to me), and it is confirmed three times
in the book of Revelation. For example:

*"I am the Alpha and the Omega, the Beginning and the
End," says the Lord, "**who is** and **who was** and **who is to
come**, the Almighty"* (Revelation 1:8).

When, through his Son, we are in a right relationship
with **Yahveh** and invoke his name, we guarantee his
involvement. We also declare to every principality and
power—in heaven, on earth, and under the earth—that
the Eternal God, the One **who ever was, is now, and ever
will be**, is our God. It is a powerful proclamation and,
in fact, we are admonished to use this majestic name of
God (here I temporarily drop the "Lord" and use God's
proper name):

*God said to Moses, "Thus you shall say to the children of
Israel: **Yahveh**, God of your fathers, the God of Abraham,
the God of Isaac, and the God of Jacob, has sent me to you.
This is my name forever, and this is my memorial to all
generations"* (Exodus 3:15).

The name **Yahveh** is more than a name, it is a **memorial**—a
"particular remembrance." It was not sufficient for God to
continue being known as *El Shaddai*, (God Almighty)—
he wanted his timelessness known:

*I appeared to Abraham, to Isaac, and to Jacob, as El
Shaddai, [God Almighty], but by my name, **Yahveh**, I was
not known to them* (Exodus 6:3).

We are enjoined to call upon God by his name **Yahveh**, but error, together with tradition, has robbed him of his proper name and us of the desire to be obedient to his wishes. However, God commands us not to use his name **Yahveh** carelessly (Deuteronomy 5: 11), which means we are to be ever respectful and reverential in its use. Using God's proper name flippantly will bring a person much sorrow.

The names **Yahveh**, and *I AM* (itself an expansion of **Yahveh**, using repetitions of ה (*heh*), י (*yod*), ה (*heh*)— three of the four letters of the Tetragrammaton)— denote the personality, individuality, self-existence, and immutability of the Divine Being who designates himself as our God, our Father, our Lord, and our Master—we would do well to remember this and treat him with the utmost respect at all times.

Dear Lord:

Thank you Father for revealing your proper name to us, the name by which you wish to be remembered. Help us to internalize your memorial name and the significance of what it means. And may we be ever mindful to your edict not to use your name carelessly for it is a memorial name, and it is holy. Amen.

Shema Yisrael!

The *Shema* is a linchpin of the Jewish faith, thousands of Jews who met a violent death at the hands of anti-Semites—even professing "Christians"—died with the *Shema* on their lips. The *Shema*, is of course:

Hear O Israel, the LORD *our God the* LORD *is* **one**
(Deuteronomy 6:4).

From right to left the Hebrew text reads:

שמע ישראל יהוה אלהינו יהוה אחד
(Deuteronomy 6:4).

I have emphasized the word "*one*" in both the English and the Hebrew. This scripture is very often used by Jews to show the perceived error of Christianity in believing its God is a deity in trifold form—*Father, Son*, and *Holy Spirit*, because it clearly states that God is **One**. Now, this "*one*" in the Hebrew text is the prime number **One**, it is not stating that God exists in only one form, and anyone who has ever read the Bible carefully will be well aware that God has many forms. Both Jews and Christians will agree that there is only one God, but disagree over what is commonly called the "trinity." Jews would rather die than accept that there is *God the Father, God the Son,* and *God the Holy Spirit.* And true Christians would rather die than allow that there is neither *God the Son* nor *God the Holy Spirit.* The two thousand-year thrust and parry has gotten violent at times, but I hope that what I write in this chapter will put an end to an issue that I feel has not been well thought out.

Compare the above *Shema* with another scripture in which the same Hebrew word "*one*" (אחד) is used. In the text below, which is well translated in the *NKJV* and *NASB*, it reads:

*But He is **unique**, and who can make Him change? And whatever His soul desires, that He does* (Job 23:13).

Reading the Hebrew text from right to left:

והוא באחד ומי ישיבנו ונפשו אותה ויעש (Job 23:13).

It is the same word (אחד), yet no English-language translator renders it as "*one*" as they have all done in Deuteronomy 6:4. And why is that? Simply because it would be rather nonsensical to do so.

Checking a number of English-language Bible versions I found something akin to waffling concerning Job 23:13, and even the *NIV's* rendering of *he stands alone* is still light years away from capturing the real essence of that which the verse is so desirous of making known.

Speaking of himself through Isaiah, God says:

*Remember the former things of old, for **I am God, and there is no other; I am God, and there is none like me*** (Isaiah 46:9).

For our purpose, in this chapter God kills two birds with one stone: he first says that there is **no other**, which should make our Jewish friends happy, and then he says: **there is none like me**, which bears out Job's statement that God is **unique**. A great man of God delivered on this verse so beautifully (emphas is mine):

God in his essential being is *unique* **in the only sense that word will bear. That is, there is nothing like him in the universe.** What he is cannot be conceived by the mind because he is **"altogether other"** than anything with which we have had experience before. **The mind has no material with which to start. No man has ever entertained a thought which can be said to describe God in any but the vaguest and most imperfect sense.** Where God is known at all it must be otherwise than by our creature reason.

A.W. Tozer – *The Divine Conquest.*

God is *sui generis*, which literally means that *he is of his own kind*. He is, literally, *unique*. Since the core meaning of *unique*—from Latin "**one**"—is "being only one of its kind," it is logically impossible to submodify it—it is either "*unique*" or it is not—there are no stages in between. This means that God cannot be described as being "virtually *unique*" or any other modification of the word. He is, literally, *unique*, one of a kind—*there is none other* of God's kind. Therefore, as we saw in the chapter entitled The Memorial Name, the LORD's name that he wishes to be known by is *Yahveh*, thus I believe Deuteronomy 6:4 should really read:

Hear O Israel, Yahveh our God, Yahveh is **unique**
(Deuteronomy 6:4).

God Almighty is *unique*; he is of his own kind; he stands alone; there is none like him. Therefore: *Hear O Israel, Yahveh our God, Yahveh is* **one of his own kind**, *Yahveh is* **unique** *and* **there is none like him**. I am firmly convinced that this is the true meaning of the *Shema*, presented to us in Deuteronomy 6:4.

Dear Lord:

Our hearts sing praise to you all the live-long day, not only for the atonement made for us by your *only begotten Son, Jesus,* or for the eternal life that is bestowed upon us for truly believing that Jesus is your Son, but our hearts also sing praise continually because you **stand alone**, there is **none like you**; you are **unique** in every essence of the word—*Hear O Church of the firstborn, Yahveh our God is Unique!* Amen.

Praise and Worship

Almost without exception, an evangelical church's Sunday bulletin will inform that there will be a time of "Praise and Worship." If there is no bulletin, it will usually be announced verbally that there will be a time of "Praise and Worship." This phrase, however, is not biblical and the real intent of the words is generally lost to members of the Church.

A true biblical phrase would be "*Thanksgiving and Praise*," and I believe we should adopt this phrase and use it regularly; if we did it would bring a great benefit to both our churches and to us as individual members of the Church.

First of all, at least half of the times we read the word "*praise*" in our Bibles we are being misled because the Hebrew word interpreted as "*praise*" is אודה (*odeh*), which means "thank." The Hebrew word for praise is הלל (*halel*). Both words can be found together:

And he [David] appointed some of the Levites to minister before the ark of the LORD, to commemorate, to thank (להדות), and to praise (להלל) the LORD God of Israel (1Chronicles 16:4). The Levites were to stand every morning to thank (להדות) and to praise (להלל) the LORD, and likewise at evening (1Chronicles 23:30).

Similarly:

In the days of David and Asaph of old there were chiefs of the singers, and songs of praise and thanksgiving to God (Nehemiah 12:46).

In General, the Church has dropped the *thanksgiving* element and substituted it with *"worship"* in which very few churches participate. Worship means **doing** something, usually lying face down, prostrate on the floor.

The biblical meaning of the word *"worship"* is a state of **doing**. What is generally translated into the English-language editions of the Bible as *"worship"* comes from the Hebrew word השתחות (*histukavot*), which literally means "to bow down," or "to prostrate oneself." This action carries over into the New Testament where we have a plethora of usages of the word *"worship;"* two examples will suffice:

*Those who were in the boat came and **worshiped** him, saying, "Truly You are the Son of God"* (Matthew 14:33).

*The eleven disciples went away into Galilee, to the mountain which Jesus had appointed for them. When they saw him, they **worshiped** him; but some doubted*
(Matthew 28:16–17).

After Jesus rebuked the sea and the waves and it became calm, those in the boat **worshiped** him. Similarly, when the disciples saw Jesus in Galilee following the resurrection *they **worshiped*** him. They did not sing songs, they **worshiped**. The Greek word used in these examples is προσεκύνησαν (*prosekunesan*), which continues with a portrait of action: "to do reverence or homage by **prostration**" … "**fall down before**" … "to bow one's self in adoration" (Mounce), "**prostrate oneself** in homage" (Strong). Throughout both the Old and New Testaments **worship** is **worship**. It is much more than the singing of songs and the clapping of hands; how many evangelical churches today allow full freedom of worship; encouraging worshipers to bow down before *God Almighty* or prostrate themselves on the church floor before the One whom they adore? True worship is vital to the spiritual life of a believer, no less so than true gratitude to him for their salvation.

Gratitude is important to God. Through our belief in Jesus we become *"children of God"* (John 1:12), and there are few parents who like ungrateful children; God is no exception. The following passage of scripture indicates how the Lord feels about ungrateful people that receive of his goodness, but give little or nothing back in the way of gratitude:

As Jesus entered a certain village, he was met by ten men who were lepers, who stood at a distance. They lifted up their voices and said, "Jesus, Master, have mercy on us!"

So when he saw them, he said to them, "Go, show yourselves to the priests." And as they went, they were cleansed.

One *of them, when he saw that he was healed, came back, and with a loud voice glorified God, and **fell down on his face at the feet of Jesus, giving him thanks.** And he was a Samaritan.*

*So Jesus responded and said, "**Were there not ten cleansed? Where are the other nine?** Were there none found who returned to give glory to God except this foreigner?"* (Luke 17:12–18).

In the above passage we catch a glimpse of God's hurt from man's ingratitude. Jesus is making a point that gratitude and having a thankful heart is important to him. We take too much for granted, and our "giving of thanks" before meals is often more of a Christian rite than of a heartfelt giving of thanks to God for his bountiful provision. "*Thanks*" and "*thanksgiving*" appear forty-six times in the New Testament; obviously, the expressing of thanks to God is very important.

The Samaritan man came back and gave glory to God. Gratitude is *coming back to say thank you to the One who literally gave himself for you*; we must never take God for granted. Unfortunately, our tradition of "praise and worship" and the translating of "praise" in place of "thanks" has robbed God of much of what is rightfully his, what is rightfully due to him for all that he has given to us, done for us, and is to us. The Lord is our Creator and he expects *thanksgiving* from his creation; we should seek him, not disappoint him:

*I will offer to you the **sacrifice of thanksgiving**, and will call upon the name of the* LORD (Psalms 116:17).

Thanksgiving can be either verbal, or as gifts offered back to him. When God allows desirable things to fall into our possession we should immediately offer them back to him in ***thanksgiving—thanksgiving*** gives glory and honor to him:

*The one who offers **thanksgiving** as his sacrifice glorifies me* (Psalms 50:23 *ESV*).

The above verse is from one English translation that does, in this instance, render the Hebrew word תודה (*todah*) correctly, almost all others render it as *praise*.

But speaking of *thanksgiving* God says:

*Now this is the law of the sacrifice of **peace offerings** which shall be presented to the* LORD. *If he offers it for a **thanksgiving**, then he shall offer, with the **sacrifice of thanksgiving**, unleavened cakes mixed with oil, unleavened wafers anointed with oil, or cakes of blended flour mixed with oil. Besides the cakes, as his offering he shall offer leavened bread with the **sacrifice of thanksgiving** of his **peace offering*** (Leviticus 7:11–13).

Through the sacrifice of his Son Jesus, God Almighty opened the way for us to be reconciled back to him through faith, receiving forgiveness and eternal life:

*Therefore, having been justified by faith, **we have peace with God** through our Lord Jesus Christ* (Romans 5:1).

*For he [Jesus] himself **is our peace**, who has made both one, and has broken down the middle wall of separation, having abolished in his flesh the enmity, that is, the law of commandments contained in ordinances, so as to create in himself one new man from the two, **thus making peace*** (Ephesians 2:14–15).

Therefore, whenever we offer *thanksgiving* to God from a grateful heart, it is also accepted as *a peace offering*. But it must be *freely* given, not offered under constraint:

*And when you offer **a sacrifice of thanksgiving** to the* LORD, ***offer it of your own free will*** (Leviticus 22:29).

In order to fully understand the importance to God of a grateful, thankful heart we should look at Psalm 118:19–20. Back in the late 1970s I was a staff member at *Orama*, a two hundred and fifty member Christian community on Great Barrier Island, a hundred miles off the coast of New Zealand. Each working day there was a group devotional time in which members were encouraged to share what the Lord had been doing in their lives. One morning I had read Psalm 118 in my private devotional time, and verses 19 and 20 were, for some inexplicable reason, burned into my soul.

Later that morning, when we had our group devotional time, the community elder who led us that day asked people to share what was on their heart. My heart was pounding. I knew it had something to do with the two verses of scripture that were running around in my head, but I did not understand them and did not want to stand up and share what I did not understand. No one shared anything, there was complete silence. And my heart was pounding so hard that I was surprised no one heard it. After about a minute of silence the elder said: "Will the person whose heart is beating so hard it is fit to burst please stand up and share what the Lord is showing him." I stood up and explained that my heart was pounding, but that I did not understand why, except for two verses of scripture that twirled and whirled about in my head, and I shared the verses. However, it was to be several years before the relevance of those verses would come crashing through into my consciousness. I share them here::

*Open to me **the gates of righteousness**, that I may enter through them **and give thanks to the Lord. This is the gate of the Lord**; the righteous shall enter through it*
(Psalm 118:19–20).

The *gates of righteousness* are *gratitude* and *thankfulness*. We enter those gates only with hearts overflowing with **gratitude** and **thankfulness** to God; only the righteous enter those **gates** and give **thanks** (תודה – *todah*)—(**not** "*praise*") to the LORD. Now look what the LORD says to us by his Spirit:

This is the gate of the LORD; *the righteous shall enter through it.*

We have gone from **gates** (plural) *of righteousness (*צדק-שערי*)*, to the singular **gate of the LORD** *(שער ליהוה).* The **righteous** go through **the gates**, but the **thankful** go through **the gate of the LORD**. Thankfulness **is** *the gate of the LORD.* Consider well these words: **thankfulness** and **gratitude** is **the gateway to the heart of God**. A grateful heart is the key to blessing and prosperity. When we are truly grateful to God for all that he is and all that he has done we have open access to the heart of God. Also, he gives us more of everything because he is assured that we will be grateful and say "thank you" for whatever he does for us, and for everything he gives to us.

The concept of gratitude to the LORD is carried over from Old Testament writings into those of the New Testament, and the established problem of interpreting "*praise*" in place of "*thanksgiving*" is also carried into the New Testament:

"*Through him then let us continually offer up **a sacrifice of praise** to God, that is, the fruit of lips that acknowledge his name*" (Hebrews 13:15).

The Greek word translated as "*praise*" in the above scripture verse occurs nowhere else in the New

Testament, it is a one-off word—αἰνέσεως (*ainesis*). Greek dictionaries note that the word means the act of praising, but "**(specially) a thank(-offering)**." The *Tyndale Commentary* for this word says: "There is a fundamental distinction in the type of sacrifices offered, for whereas Christ offered himself, the believer is to offer a sacrifice of thanksgiving to God. This idea of *thanksgiving* is frequent in the New Testament and may in fact be regarded as *the norm for Christians*. Especially characteristic is the idea that such a sacrifice should be offered continually – διὰ παντὸς (*dia pantos*) – in striking contrast to the once-for-all character of the sacrifice of Christ."

The commentator clearly acknowledges that the one-off use of this word means "*thanksgiving*" more than "*praise*." Why cannot translators understand this and translate accordingly? Tradition!

I agree most wholeheartedly with the *Tyndale* commentator that there "is a fundamental distinction in the type of sacrifices offered," there is αἶνον (*ainos*) "*praise*" and there is εὐχαριστοῦντες, (*eucharisteo*) which is "*thanks*." And in our scripture from Hebrews we have αἰνέσεως (*ainesis*), which is more than "*praise*" and more than "*thanks*," it is αἰνέσεως (*ainesis*), a special "*thank-offering*." The point is that we should "continually offer up a sacrifice" of *thanksgiving* to God, the *fruit* of our hearts.

We are continually exhorted to offer thanks to God:

giving thanks always for all things to God the Father in the name of our Lord Jesus Christ (Ephesians 5:20).

We are told not to be anxious about anything, but to make our needs known to God along with *thanksgiving*:

*Be anxious for nothing, but in everything by prayer and supplication, **with thanksgiving**, let your requests be made known to God* (Philippians 4:6).

Spontaneous, heartfelt *giving of thanks* (Ephesians 5:4) is essential to a full orbed life as a believer in and as a priest unto the Lord.

Some believers do appear to be blessed more than others. And I think it is safe to identify this group as those who have truly grateful hearts, who, when the Lord gives them a gift are profuse in their gratitude. Then the Lord apparently says, "What a nice child. Here, have some more!"

As we have seen, church members generally do not "*worship*" in the biblical sense so we should adjust our order of church services and make room for times of real "*Thanksgiving and Praise.*"

Dear Lord:
Help us Lord to cultivate a *thankful* and *grateful* heart. Cause us to offer real *thanksgiving* for all that is put upon our tables at mealtimes. We are reminded that when Jesus gave thanks for the loaves and fishes that he divided among thousands, that he did more than say "Thank you." He *blessed* the food, and the Greek word used for "*blessed*" is εὐλόγησε (*eulogeo*), from which we get our word eulogy, meaning "to speak well of." May we learn from our Lord to speak well of the abundance of food that we so much take for granted. Similarly, let us

cultivate a ***thankful*** and ***grateful*** heart for all that comes to us in the way of goods and clothing:

Every good gift and every perfect gift is from above, and comes down from the Father *of lights, with whom there is no variation or shadow of turning* (James 1:17).

May we learn what "**appreciation**" really means. Amen.

Absent from the Body

The following topic is bound to be a contentious one for some readers and is sure to raise a few hackles in various circles; however, as I said at the close of an earlier chapter, readers must make their own judgments according to the evidence of Scripture presented. Readers should provoke their minds to think out rationally what their minds accept easily, and without thought.

I would like to make it very clear at the outset that I am only presenting scriptural fact as I understand it, not attempting to promote a doctrine. I strongly suggest that readers emulate the people of Berea who: *searched the Scriptures daily to find out whether these things were so* (Acts 17:11). It is often a difficult and lonely task to present truth that others may not wish to hear.

There is a multitude of believers who have had glimpses into heaven or hell, and many have been comforted by seeing loved ones who had passed away. I would argue that these happenings were visions, not actual events, but which appear as real as life itself. I have been privileged to have had two visions and they were both breathtakingly awesome in their reality, so real that decades later I can virtually recall every detail. Our gracious God gives visions in order to warn, to comfort, to instruct, or to simply show us that the world beyond ours is so very, very real. The apostle Paul writes of an experience he had:

*I will come to **visions** and revelations of the Lord: I know a man in Christ who fourteen years ago—**whether in the body I do not know, or whether out of the body I do not know, God knows**—such a one was caught up to the third heaven. And I know such a man—**whether in the body or out of the body I do not know, God knows**—how he was caught up into **Paradise** and heard inexpressible words, which it is not lawful for a man to utter*

(2Corinthians 12:1–4).

For Paul, the vision was so real that he did not know whether he was in or out of his body. The apostle Peter had a somewhat similar type of experience:

*Now behold, an angel of the Lord stood by him, and a light shone in the prison; and he struck Peter on the side and raised him up, saying, "Arise quickly!" And his chains fell off his hands. Then the angel said to him, "Gird yourself and tie on your sandals"; and so he did. And he said to him, "Put on your garment and follow me." So he went out and followed him, and **did not know that what was done by the angel was real, but thought he was seeing a vision*** (Acts 12:7–9).

Three people in the Bible are shown not to have died in the usual fashion of mortals. Two of these, Moses and Elijah, were with Jesus when the Son of God was transfigured on the summit of Mount Tabor. Peter, James, and John clearly saw the three talking together and wanted to build three tabernacles there, one each for Jesus, Moses, and Elijah (Matthew 17:4).

The third person was Enoch who walked with God and whom God translated straight from the realm of the physical to that of the spiritual (Genesis 5:24).

The Bible informs us that Moses died in the presence of God on Mount Nebo (later called Pisgah), and by way of explanation for the lack of a body tells us that God buried him and that no one knows where that grave is (Deuteronomy 34:6).

We also read that Elijah was taken up by a whirlwind into heaven ((2kings 2:11). Thus we have three men of God who went directly from this physical world into the spiritual world—into heaven; however, these accounts are very far from the norm and it is rather foolish to base upon them the widely-held Christian belief that immediately at the moment of death a Christian is ushered directly into the presence of the Lord. The Bible narrative does not appear to support such a doctrine.

We must thrust tradition aside and proceed to fairly examine all passages relating to death, resurrection, and the entrance into glory if we are to arrive at a more definitive answer of what takes place at death.

The great apostle Paul wrote to the Corinthians something that has since become a mantra for many believers:

*We are confident, yes, well pleased rather to be **absent from the body and to be present with the Lord***
(2Corinthians 5:8).

However, Paul wrote a great deal about the body, the "*tent*" in which we live and the desire to put off this "*tent*" for a permanent home in heaven, but we must carefully consider all of his writings on the subject. Before we do that, let us back up to where our Lord spoke pointedly to one of the thieves being crucified along with himself, something which millions have since grasped like a buoyancy aid in a shipwreck without having given it much thought at all:

*One of the thieves who were being hanged railed at Jesus, saying, "If you are Christ, save yourself and us." The other, answering, rebuked him, saying, "Do you not fear God, seeing that you are under the same condemnation? And we indeed rightly, for we are receiving the just reward for our deeds; but this man has done nothing wrong." He said to Jesus, "Lord, **remember me when you come into your kingdom**." Jesus said to him, "Truly, **I say to you today, you will be with me in Paradise**"* (Luke 23:39–43).

The sentence spoken by Jesus to the thief has been used to undergird the belief in an event that is patently obvious that it did not take place that day. The false belief is that both Jesus and the thief entered *Paradise* (heaven) that day, but this cannot possibly be. It is grasping at straws. It is the placement of the comma that has led to such a belief, but there is no such comma in the classical Greek texts; however, a comma has been placed **before** the word "*today*" in modern Greek texts simply because tradition requires it. The thief asked Jesus to *remember* him "*when you come into your kingdom*." The repentant thief had no expectation of being taken to heaven that day, he simply asked to be *remembered* when Jesus came to take up his throne.

Virtually at the close of my writing on this topic I consulted eight distinguished commentaries in order to view their findings; there was no consensus of opinion. An Eighteenth century commentator, a British Methodist minister, seemingly blew a fuse over the possibility that "men of great learning and abilities" attempt to place a comma after σημερον (*today*), which means he did not even entertain the fact that Jesus **descended** after death, not **ascended** to *Paradise* (a Persian word meaning a walled garden). One commentator expressed the view that the repentant thief was "prepared for a long delay" before Jesus came to take up his throne. Others simply beat around the bush with this obvious religious hot potato, not wanting to commit themselves one way or the other because of the controversial nature of the topic. But let us look logically at facts that may dispel the false hopes of many:

*A wicked and adulterous generation seeks after a sign, and no sign shall be given to it except **the sign of the prophet Jonah*** (Matthew 16:4).

*For **as Jonah was three days and three nights in the fish's belly, so will the Son of Man be three days and three nights in the heart of the earth*** (Matthew 12:40).

Jesus was three days and nights in the heart of the earth, in the netherworld, the underworld of the dead; some refer to it as "*hell.*" That, by any stretch of the imagination, cannot be considered to be "*Paradise.*" The fact that Jesus was dead and descended into the heart of the earth for three days and nights is one of the foundational truths of Christianity. Jesus did not rise from the dead until the third day:

*thus it was necessary for Christ to suffer, and **to rise from the dead on the third day*** (Luke 24:46).

*God **raised him up on the third day**, and showed Him openly* (Acts 10:40).

*Now may the God of peace who **brought up our Lord Jesus from the dead**, that great Shepherd of the sheep, through the blood of the everlasting covenant, make you complete in every good work...* (Hebrews 13:20–21).

Jesus was raised on the third day, but during those days Jesus did not remain in the tomb, he **descended** into the netherworld, the realm of the dead, and it was from there that **Jesus was brought up**, thus we have:

*"Who will descend into the abyss?" (that is, **to bring Christ up from the dead**)* – (Romans 10:7).

*Now that **he ascended**, what is it but that he also **descended first into the lower parts of the earth?*** (Ephesians 4:9).

Jesus told the repentant thief that he **would be with him in Paradise**, but following that Jesus **descended** into the netherworld and **did not rise for three days**, which makes it impossible for the repentant thief to have been in *Paradise* with Jesus that same day. Of a consequence there must be a different interpretation of what Jesus is held to have said, because the reformed thief certainly did not go straight to heaven(*Paradise*) with Jesus.

As with all the dead the spirit remains alive, and Jesus was very much alive in the Spirit when he descended into the netherworld—the underworld of the dead—and preached the gospel to its inhabitants:

*Christ also suffered once for sins, the just for the unjust, that he might bring us to God, being put to death in the flesh but **made alive by the Spirit, by whom** he also went **and preached to the spirits in prison**, who formerly were disobedient* (1Peter 3:18–19).

For this reason **the gospel was preached also to those who are dead, that they might be judged according to men in the flesh,** *but live according to God in the spirit* (1Peter 4:6).

The thief had repented and had been accepted by Jesus. Jesus descended into *"hell"* and gave the gospel to its residents; however, the former thief did not get raised from the grave **before** Jesus, so we can also rule that out:

Christ … would be **the first to rise from the dead** (Acts 26:23).

He [Jesus] is **the … firstborn from the dead** (Colossians 1:18).

Jesus Christ, the faithful witness, **the firstborn from the dead** (Revelation 1:5).

Having established that Jesus did not enter *Paradise* (return to heaven) on the day of his crucifixion; and also having established that the forgiven thief did not rise from the dead before Jesus, we must now consider the state of being dead and what it means. With rare exceptions, like Enoch, Moses, and Elijah, all whose heart stops beating and lungs no longer bring oxygen into the bloodstream, are defined by the medical profession as being *"dead,"* but that is not the biblical definition. The Bible also states clearly that:

It is appointed for men to die once, **but after this** *the judgment* (Hebrews 9:27).

And I saw **the dead,** *small and great, standing before God, and books were opened. And another book was opened,* *which is the Book of Life. And **the dead were judged** according to their works, by the things which were written in the books* (Revelation 20:12).

Therefore, if a person is to be judged after he has died, that person cannot be truly dead as we understand the word. There must, of necessity, be a state between *death* and *judgment*. The New Testament unequivocally teaches us that there is **no condemnation for those who are in Christ Jesus** (Romans 8:1). But Jesus also made it clear that those who do not believe in him are already **dead** even while they yet draw breath:

*But Jesus said to him, "Follow Me, and **let the dead bury their own dead**"* (Matthew 8:22).

Jude goes further again; he speaks of former members of the Church who have gone back into the world as being "***twice dead***" (Jude 12). And besides, all those who do not have an intimate, personal, and vital relationship with the Lord Jesus Christ will face death **a second time**:

*He who has an ear, let him hear what the Spirit says to the churches. The one who conquers will not be hurt by **the second death*** (Revelation 2:11).

*Blessed and holy is the one **who shares in the first resurrection! Over such the second death has no power**, but they will be priests of God and of Christ, and they will reign with him for a thousand years* (Revelation 20:6).

*Then Death and Hades were thrown into the lake of fire. This is **the second death, the lake of fire***

(Revelation 20:14).

*But as for the **cowardly**, the **faithless**, the **detestable**, as for **murderers**, the **sexually immoral**, **sorcerers**, **idolaters**,*

and all **liars**, *their portion will be in the lake that burns with fire and sulfur,* **which is the second death**
(Revelation 21:8).

So now we come back and address the state between *death* and *resurrection*; between *death* and *judgment*; between the *first death* and the *second death*. In the Bible this state is described as *"sleep."* Sometimes, Jesus personally intervened and woke young and old alike from their *"sleep;"* those who were considered by many to have been *"dead"*:

When [Jesus] came into the house of the ruler of the synagogue, he allowed no one to go in except Peter, and James, and John, and the father and the mother of the young girl. All wept and lamented for her, but he said, "Why do you make such a tumult? Do not weep, she is not dead, but **sleeping.***" And they laughed him to scorn,* **knowing that she was dead.** *He put them all out and entered in where the young girl was lying. He took the young girl by the hand, and said to her, "Talitha cumi," which is, being interpreted, "Little girl, arise."* **Her spirit returned,** *and she got up straight away and walked, for she was twelve years of age* (Luke8:51–55).

These things Jesus said, and after that he said to them, "Our friend **Lazarus sleeps,** *but I go that* **I may wake him up.***" Then His disciples said, "Lord,* **if he sleeps he will get well.***" However,* **Jesus spoke of his death,** *but they thought that he was speaking about* **taking rest in sleep.** *Then Jesus said to them plainly, "***Lazarus is dead***"*
(John 11:11–14).

*Now when He had said these things, he cried with a loud voice, "**Lazarus, come forth!**" And he who had **died** came out bound hand and foot with grave clothes, and his face was wrapped with a cloth. Jesus said to them, "Loose him, and let him go." (John 11:43–44).*

The apostle Paul writes to the Christians in Corinth and mentions that some of the disciples who had seen Jesus after his resurrection had fallen *asleep* (died):

*I delivered to you first of all that which I also received: that Christ died for our sins according to the Scriptures, and that he **was buried**, and that he **rose again the third day** according to the Scriptures, and that he was seen by Cephas [Peter], then by the twelve [disciples]. **After that he was seen by over five hundred brethren at once**, of whom the greater part remain to the present, but **some have fallen asleep [died]**. After that he was seen by James, then by all the apostles. Then last of all he was seen by me also, as by one born out of due time*

(1 Corinthians 15:4–8).

So the biblical term for those who have *died* is that they are *"sleeping."* This is not restricted just to the New Testament, the Old Testament also shows us this. Fearing his enemies, King Saul disguised himself, went to a medium, and asked her to call the prophet Samuel up from the dead, which she did:

*Now Samuel said to Saul, "**Why have you disturbed me by bringing me up?**" And Saul answered, "I am deeply distressed; for the Philistines make war against me, and God has departed from me and does not answer me anymore, neither by prophets nor by dreams. Therefore **I***

have summoned you, *that you may reveal to me what I should do*" (1Samuel 28:15).

Here we see Samuel describing his being brought up as being **disturbed** from sleep. Calling up the dead was an abomination in the eyes of the Lord and he commanded:

*There shall not be found among you anyone who makes his son or his daughter pass through the fire, or one who practices witchcraft, or a soothsayer, or one who interprets omens, or a sorcerer, or one who conjures spells, or a medium, or a spiritist, **or one who calls up the dead**. For all who do these things are an abomination to the Lord* (Deuteronomy 18:10–12).

People are not "*dead*," they are only *sleeping*, and they shall all be resurrected; this is also taught in both the Old and the New Testaments:

*And multitudes of those who **sleep** in the dust of the earth shall awake, **some to everlasting life, some to shame and everlasting contempt*** (Daniel 12:2).

*The hour is coming in which **all who are in the graves** will hear [Jesus'] voice and come forth—those who have done good, to **the resurrection of life**, and those who have done evil, to **the resurrection of condemnation*** (John 5:28).

And when will the *resurrection* take place? *At the Last Day*:

*This is the will of the Father who sent me, that of all he has given me I should lose nothing, but should **raise it up at the last day*** (John 6:39).

*And this is the will of him who sent me, that everyone who sees the Son and believes in him may have everlasting life; and I will raise him up **at the last day*** (John 6:40).

*Whoever eats my flesh and drinks my blood has eternal life, and I will raise him up **at the last day*** (John 6:54).

*No man can come to me except the Father who sent me draws him, and **I will raise him up at the last day*** (John 6:44).

*Jesus said to [Martha], "Your brother **will rise again**." Martha said to him, "I know that he will rise again **in the resurrection at the last day**." Jesus said to her, "I am the resurrection and the life. He who believes in me, **though he may die, he shall live**. And whoever lives and believes in me **shall never die**"* (John 11:23–26).

When is **the last day** for true believers? The Scriptures indicate that it is at the coming of Christ:

*But now Christ is risen from the dead, and has become the firstfruits of **those who have fallen asleep**. For since by man came death, by Man also came the resurrection of the dead. For as in Adam **all die, even so [all] in Christ all shall be made alive**. But each one in his own order: Christ the firstfruits, **afterward those who are Christ's at his coming*** (1Corinthians 15:20-23).

All those who belong to Christ will be resurrected at his return, but not resurrected into the likeness of the former body. Jairus' twelve-year-old daughter was "***known***" to be *dead*, but the moment Jesus said, "*Little girl, arise*." **Her spirit returned**, *and she got up* (Luke 8:54–55). In the case of Lazarus, when Jesus called out: "**Lazarus,** *come forth!"* Lazarus came out (John 11:43–44). When Jesus had compassion for the widow in Nain who had lost her only son, he touched the coffin and said, *"Young man, I say to you, arise." So* **he who was dead sat up** *and began to speak* (Luke 7:14–15).

The above three examples (there were probably many more) showed the **dead** came back to life on earth in their own bodies. But when Jesus calls all those who are sleeping (**dead**) out of their graves it will not be to a life on earth and they will not arise in their old bodies. In the Bible angels appeared and disappeared at will, and Jesus said that we shall be like **angels of God in heaven** (Matthew 22:30). Jesus just appeared in rooms, ate **fish** and **honeycomb** (Luke 24:42), and he was not just Spirit, because he said to the disciples:

See my hands and my feet, that it is I myself. **Touch me, and see. For a spirit does not have flesh and bones** *as you see that I have* (Luke 24:39).

And does not the Scripture tell us:

We are children of God; and it has not yet been revealed what we shall be, but we know that **when he is revealed, we shall be like him** (1John 3:2).

For our citizenship is in heaven, from which we also eagerly wait for the Savior, **the Lord Jesus Christ, who will transform our lowly body that it may be conformed to His glorious body** (Philippians 3:20–21).

The apostle Paul provides us with a great deal more information to muse upon; what we shall be like and how it will take place:

But someone will say, "How are the dead raised up? And with what body do they come?" Foolish one, **what you sow is not made alive unless it dies**. And **what you sow, you do not sow that body that shall be**, but mere grain— perhaps wheat or some other grain. But **God gives it a body as he pleases, and to each seed its own body.**

All flesh is not the same flesh, but there is one kind of flesh of men, another flesh of animals, another of fish, and another of birds.

There are also celestial bodies and terrestrial bodies; but the glory of the celestial is one, and the glory of the terrestrial is another. There is one glory of the sun, another glory of the moon, and another glory of the stars; for one star differs from another star in glory.

So also is the resurrection of the dead. The body is sown in corruption, it is raised in incorruption. It is sown in dishonor, **it is raised in glory**. It is sown in weakness, **it is raised in power**. It is sown a natural body, **it is raised a spiritual body**. There is a natural body, and there is a spiritual body. And so it is written, "The first man Adam became a living being." The last Adam became a life-giving spirit.

However, the spiritual is not first, but the natural, and afterward the spiritual. The first man was of the earth, made of dust; the second Man is the Lord from heaven. As was the man of dust, so also are those who are made of dust; and as is the heavenly Man, so also are those who are heavenly. And as we have borne the image of the man of dust, we shall also **bear the image of the heavenly Man.**

Now this I say, brethren, that flesh and blood cannot inherit the kingdom of God; nor does corruption inherit *incorruption. Behold, I tell you a mystery:* **We shall not all sleep**, *but we* **shall all be changed**—*in a moment, in the twinkling of an eye,* **at the last trumpet**. *For the trumpet will sound, and* **the dead will be raised incorruptible**, *and we shall be changed* (1Corinthians 15:35–52).

We finally arrive back at Paul's "*tent*," his earthly body mentioned near the beginning of this piece. The body is described as a "*tent*" because it is a temporary dwelling, our permanent dwelling will come with the *resurrection*. Peter also uses "*tent*" as a metaphor for his body and that he will soon leave it (be martyred):

I think it is right, **as long as I am in this tent**, *to stir you up by reminding you, knowing that* **shortly I must put off my tent**, *just as our Lord Jesus Christ showed me*
(2Peter 1:13–14).

Paul explains that the body, **our earthly house**, is a "*tent*," and that if it is destroyed we have a building from God, a house not made with hands, eternal in the heavens. And then Paul tells us that he longs to be clothed with his permanent house from heaven, and that he does not want to be found "*naked*," in the state between dying and resurrection, he does not **want to be unclothed, but further clothed, that mortality may be swallowed up by life**. In other words, Paul longed for what is known as the Rapture, when his mortality would be swallowed up by eternal life:

For we know that if **our earthly house, this tent**, *is destroyed, we have a building from God, a house not made with hands, eternal in the heavens. For in this we groan, earnestly desiring to be clothed with our habitation which*

*is from heaven, if indeed, **having been clothed, we shall
not be found naked. For we who are in this tent groan,**
being burdened, **not because we want to be unclothed,
but further clothed, that mortality may be swallowed
up by life*** (2Corinthians 5:1–4).

Paul elucidates even further. His greatest desire is to be
raptured out of his body and be eternally with the Lord.
He so much wants what many of us dearly desire—an
Enoch experience!

*So we are always confident, knowing that **while we are
at home in the body we are absent from the Lord**. For
we walk by faith, not by sight. We are confident, yes, **well
pleased rather to be absent from the body and to be
present with the Lord*** (2Corinthians 5:6–8).

Paul makes it absolutely clear that those who are alive
at the time Jesus returns, they will not get to heaven
(*Paradise*) **ahead of those who are sleeping**; we all go
together:

*For this we say to you by the word of the Lord, that **we
who are alive and remain until the coming of the Lord
will by no means precede those who are asleep**. For the
Lord himself will descend from heaven with a shout, with
the voice of an archangel, and **with the trumpet of God.
And the dead in Christ will rise first.** Then **we who are
alive and remain shall be caught up together with them**
in the clouds **to meet the Lord in the air. And thus we
shall always be with the Lord.** Therefore comfort one
another with these words.*

*But concerning the times and the seasons, brethren,
you have no need that I should write to you. For **you***

yourselves know perfectly that the day of the Lord so comes as a thief in the night. For when they say, "Peace and safety!" then sudden destruction comes upon them, as labor pains upon a pregnant woman
                    (1 Thessalonians 4:15–18, 5:1–3).

"But," you may say, "there is a scripture that says Jesus will return, bringing the Christians that have died with him." Okay, let us look at the scripture. It does not say what translators want us to believe:

*And may the Lord make you increase and abound in love to one another and to all, just as we do to you, so that he may establish your hearts blameless in holiness before our God and Father **at the coming of our Lord Jesus Christ with all his saints*** (1 Thessalonians 3:12–13).

The word interpreted as *"saints"* is the Greek word ἁγίων (*hagios*), which is in plural form and means *"holy."*

NASB Notes give *"holy ones"* as an alternative reading to *"saints,"* while the NIV correctly translates it as *"holy ones"* and cross-references it with:

*God is just: He will pay back trouble to those who trouble you and give relief to you who are troubled, and to us as well. This will happen when the Lord Jesus is revealed from heaven in blazing fire **with his powerful angels***
                    (2 Thessalonians 1:6–7 NIV).

The New King James gives us:

*When the Son of Man comes in His glory, **and all the holy angels with Him***... (Matthew 25:31) – So also the Hebrew New Testament translation.

To that we must also add two more verses from Matthew:

*For the Son of Man **is going to come with his angels** in the glory of his Father, and then he will repay each person according to what he has done* (Matthew 16:27).

*And he will **send his angels with a great sound of a trumpet**, and they will gather together his elect **from the four winds, from one end of heaven to the other*** (Matthew 24:31).

*For whoever is ashamed of me and my words in this adulterous and sinful generation, of him the Son of Man also will be ashamed when he comes in the glory of his Father **with the holy angels*** (Mark 8:38).

So, okay, how do we explain Hebrews 12:1, a passage many Christians cling to?:

*Therefore we also, **since we are surrounded by so great a cloud of witnesses**, let us lay aside every weight, and the sin which so easily ensnares us, and let us run with endurance the race that is set before us* (Hebrews 12:1).

Who are these witnesses? They are depicted in Hebrews Chapter 11. They are witnesses to their "*faith*," they are not looking down at us as from a balcony. Exactly what does Hebrews Chapter 11 tell us?:

*By **faith** Abraham, when he was tested, offered up Isaac … of whom it was said, "In Isaac your seed shall be called."*

*By **faith** Isaac blessed Jacob and Esau concerning things to come.*

*By **faith** Jacob, when he was dying, blessed each of the sons of Joseph, and worshiped, leaning on the top of his staff.*

*By **faith** Moses, when he was born, was hidden three months by his parents.*

*By **faith** Moses, when he became of age, refused to be called the son of Pharaoh's daughter.*

*By **faith** they passed through the Red Sea as by dry land, whereas the Egyptians, attempting to do so, were drowned.*

*By **faith** the walls of Jericho fell down after they were encircled for seven days.*

*By **faith** the harlot Rahab did not perish with those who did not believe, when she had received the spies with peace.*

*And what more shall I say? For the time would fail me to tell of **Gideon** and **Barak** and **Samson** and **Jephthah**, also of **David** and **Samuel** and **the prophets**: who **through faith** subdued kingdoms, worked righteousness, obtained promises, stopped the mouths of lions, quenched the violence of fire, escaped the edge of the sword, out of weakness were made strong, became valiant in battle, turned to flight the armies of the aliens. Women received their dead raised to life again.*

*Others were tortured, **not accepting deliverance, that they might obtain a better resurrection**. Still others had **trial of mockings** and **scourgings**, yes, and **of chains and imprisonment**. They were **stoned**, they were **sawn in two, were tempted**, were **slain with the sword**. They **wandered about in sheepskins and goatskins, being destitute, afflicted, tormented**—of whom the world was not worthy. They **wandered in deserts and mountains, in dens and caves of the earth*** (Hebrews 11:32–38).

And then comes the punchline:

*And all these, having obtained a good testimony through faith, **did not receive the promise, God having provided something better for us, that they should not be made perfect apart from us** (Hebrews 11:39).*

Hebrews Chapter 11 is all about faith:

*These **all died in faith, not having received the promises, but having seen them afar off were assured of them, embraced them** and confessed that they were strangers and pilgrims on the earth (Hebrews 11:13).*

There will be a clarion call from Jesus **on the last day** (John 6:40, 44, 54) and they will be resurrected. For them it will be like waking from a sound, refreshing sleep. The fortunate few, like Enoch, Moses and Elijah, bypass the dying process, but those who remain on earth at the time of the Second Coming of Jesus will experience the same upward call as the fortunate few just mentioned. Death is not something to be afraid of; as the light of physical life begins to fade, the hope of every truly twice-born child of God kicks in:

*God both raised up the Lord and **will also raise us up** by His power (1Corinthians 6:14).*

*For if we live, we live to the Lord; and if we die, we die to the Lord. Therefore, **whether we live or die, we are the Lord's**. For to this end Christ died and rose and lived again, that He might be **Lord of both the dead and the living** (Romans 14:8–9).*

*But you have come to Mount Zion and to the city of the living God, the heavenly Jerusalem, and to innumerable angels in festal gathering, and to **the general assembly of*** *the church of the firstborn who are enrolled in heaven, and to God, the judge of all, and to **the spirits of the righteous made perfect** (Hebrews 12:22–23)*

We, who have a vital, personal relationship with the Lord Jesus Christ are already registered in heaven; enrolled as members of the Church of the Firstborn. When Jesus returns we will all be raised together, constituting a General Assembly of believers *from every tribe and tongue and people and nation* (Revelation 5:9). We will all experience the same joy and euphoria at seeing the One whom we love and adore at the same time. And:

God will wipe away every tear from their eyes; there shall be no more death, nor sorrow, nor crying. There shall be no more pain, for the former things have passed away
(Revelation 21:4).

Some believers mourn the loss of their beloved children; however, a clear example of believing children not really being lost is found in the book of Job, which should put minds at rest and ease the pain:

*There was a man in the land of Uz, whose name was Job; and that man was blameless and upright, and one who feared God and shunned evil. And **seven sons and three daughters were born to him**. Also, his possessions were **seven thousand sheep, three thousand camels, five hundred yoke of oxen, five hundred female donkeys***
(Job 1:1–3).

Probably the majority of readers know the story of Job. How calamity followed catastrophe, which was followed by unmitigated disaster—until Job had lost everything—possessions, children, even his own health. Fortunately the story does not end there. We skip over forty-one interesting chapters and see that in the end *God Almighty* restored the fortunes of Job:

*Now the Lord blessed the latter days of Job more than his beginning; for he had **fourteen thousand sheep, six thousand camels, one thousand yoke of oxen, and one thousand female donkeys**. He also had **seven sons and three daughters** (Job 42:12–13).*

Job's fortunes were restored. He had **twice** as many *sheep*, **twice** as many *camels*, **twice** as many *oxen* and **twice** as many *female donkeys*. But he only had his seven sons and three daughters replaced. Why was that? Because his original sons and daughters were God-fearing (Job 1:5) and were not lost, they were *sleeping* in the spirit, waiting for their awakening at the *resurrection*. Remember this one thing:

*He is **not the God of the dead but of the living, for all live to Him** (Luke 20:38).*

*Through the Holy Spirit we have all been **sealed for the day of redemption** (Ephesians 4:30).*

Dear Lord:
Help us to look carefully at all the Scriptures concerning death and resurrection. Help us to be fully persuaded in our own minds about those events that must come to almost every man and every woman who have ever walked on this earth. Help us to understand that death is not a thing to be feared; that it is a momentary transition from one state to another; that beloved children are not

lost; that God in his compassion and love has something better for us than we can possibly imagine. Help us to look forward with hope-filled expectation and press toward the goal for *the prize of the upward call of God in Christ Jesus* (Philippians 3:14). Amen.

Jacob and Israel

It is traditionally understood that the name "*Israel*" means "Prince with God," but I do not think that this is the only possible interpretation. "*Israel*" in Hebrew is ישראל (*Yisrael*), and like many names in the Bible it is a two-part name. Certainly, שר (*sar*) means "Prince" or "Ruler," but was this what was in the mind of God Almighty when he renamed Jacob as Israel?

Practically every Bible student understands that "*el*," the last syllable in the name *Israel*, means "*God*," but most would not be aware that the first two syllables "*Isra*" (*Yisra*) come directly from the Hebrew word ישר (*yashar*), which means "straight." When we place the two parts of the name together: ישר אל (reading from right to left) it is easily seen as forming ישראל (*Israel*).

First we must look at Jacob's birth:

And the Lord said to her [Rebekah]:
   "Two nations are in your womb,
   Two peoples shall be separated from your body;
   One people shall be stronger than the other,
   *And **the older shall serve the younger**."*
   *So when her days were fulfilled for her to give birth, indeed there were twins in her womb. And the first came out red. He was like a hairy garment all over; so they called his name Esau. **Afterward his brother came out, and his hand took hold of Esau's heel; so his name was called Jacob*** (Genesis 25:23–26).

Jacob (יעקב – *Ya'acov*) comes from עקב (*akav*), the
Hebrew word for "heel," this was because he took hold
of Esau's heel at birth. Jacob (יעקב – *Ya'acov*) means
"overreacher" / "supplanter" / "grasping."

Jacob (יעקב – *Ya'acov*) certainly lived up to his
name; in his youth he excelled at being both a supplanter
and at being grasping. But he also showed that he had
a heart for God Almighty, and God made promises of
blessing to him. Whenever the Lord spoke to Jacob
(יעקב – *Ya'acov*), he would invariably set up a pillar and
anoint it:

*Then Jacob rose early in the morning, and took the stone
that he had put at his head,* **set it up as a pillar, and
poured oil on top of it** (Genesis 28:18).

*So Jacob set up a pillar in the place where [God] talked
with him,* **a pillar of stone; and he poured a drink
offering on it, and he poured oil on it** (Genesis 35:14).

At one point Jacob (יעקב – *Ya'acov*) wrestled all night
with a divine being:

*Jacob was left alone; and a Man wrestled with him until
the breaking of day. Now when he saw that he did not
prevail against him,* **he touched the socket of his hip; and
the socket of Jacob's hip was out of joint as he wrestled
with him.** *And he said, "Let me go, for the day breaks."*

*But he said, "I will not let you go unless you bless
me!" So He said to him, "What is your name?" He said,
"Jacob." And he said, "Your name shall no longer be called
Jacob, but Israel; for* **you have struggled with God and
with men, and have prevailed**" (Genesis 32:24–28).

So we find that God Almighty tells Jacob (יעקב –
Ya'acov), that he would no longer be called Jacob (יעקב
– *Ya'acov*)—"overreacher" / "supplanter" / "grasping,"
but Israel – (ישראל – *Yisrael*), "Straightened of God";
that was his blessing. The hip of Jacob (יעקב – *Ya'acov*)
was now permanently out of place—he would never walk
the same way again, and he made no further grasping
deals and supplanted no one else from that day onward;
his rough edges were now smoothed. I believe that
Jacob (יעקב – *Ya'acov*), became *Israel* ישראל (*Yisrael*):
"Straightened of God".

    Putting the names Jacob (יעקב – *Ya'acov*) and *Israel*
(ישראל – *Yisrael*) into context we have something that
was inherently **crooked** and **rough** being straightened
and smoothed out by God. I am of the opinion that
Israel – (ישראל – *Yisrael*), could just as easily mean
"Straightened of God" as "Prince with God." And
"Straightened of God" fits in with Bible prophecy:

*Every valley shall be exalted and every mountain and hill
brought low; the **crooked** places shall be made **straight**
and the **rough** places **smooth*** (Isaiah 40:4).

That is my opinion. But it has not been chiseled in stone.

Dear Lord:
Jacob wrestled **with you** and as a result limped for
the rest of his life. Help us to wrestle **before you** for
souls, and for ourselves to *put on the new man that
was created according to God, in true righteousness and
holiness* (Ephesians 4:24), that we may *walk before* you
and be blameless (Genesis 17:1), having been ourselves
"*straightened by God*." Amen.

Pray for the Peace of Jerusalem

A s I have written elsewhere, prayers, when made in the will of God, accomplishes great things, but when done outside of his will it accomplishes nothing. Thus, when Christians *pray for the peace of Jerusalem*, they are out of the LORD's will because Scripture never commands us to do this. Yes, there is definitely a verse in our English-language versions of the Bible that reads:

Pray for the peace of Jerusalem: *may they prosper who love you* (Psalms 122:6).

I consider this to be an extremely poor example of the translation of Hebrew text. In previous chapters, I have said enough about tradition and incorrect, misleading translations of the Bible to start a holy war, and I really do not want to be caught in the crossfire by touching one of the most oft-quoted, almost sacred, verses in the Scriptures, but a man has to do what a man has to do.

Pray for the peace of Jerusalem is a "traditional" interpretation that is way off base. It is, as they say in Yiddish, a *bubbemeiser*—a grandmother's story. It is so much part of Church tradition that no Bible manufacturer would dare to change it now even if they knew the correct way to translate it, which is doubtful, because most translators do not possess the understanding of the Psalm's background. Over a period of many centuries literally millions upon millions of Christians have prayed for the "Peace of Jerusalem," but Jerusalem has been sacked and destroyed ninety-one times. It has been said that, "if blood were indelible, Jerusalem would be red, all red."

Does this then mean that prayer does not work? Of course not! It means that praying for Jerusalem's peace is not on God Almighty's agenda in our day and age, nor was it in all the previous ages since David and Solomon's time. I will try to explain this, but readers will need to stay with me.

There is nothing wrong with the latter part of Psalms 122:6, "*may they prosper who love you;*" it is perfectly correct. But the first portion, in Hebrew, is (reading from right to left): שאלו שלום ירולשם (*Shalu Shlom Yerushalayim*). The Hebrew word שאלו (*shalu*) comes from the verb שאל (*sha'al*) and should never be translated as "*pray*"—ever! Of the one hundred and sixty-eight occurrences of the word שאל (*sha'al*) in the Hebrew Scriptures, the early translators chose only to translate שאל (*sha'al*) in Psalms 122:6 as "*pray*," this could only have been done through an ignorance of the phrase. In every other instance they translated שאל (*sha'al*) correctly: as "ask," "inquire," "request," "salute" (greet), etc.

On the other hand, the Hebrew word for "*pray*" is the verb פלל (*palal*), and in each of the eighty-three instances where it occurs in the Hebrew Scriptures, it is translated correctly as "*pray*," "*intercede*" (in prayer) or "*supplicate*" (in prayer). So, what does all this mean? The answer is quite simple really: Most readers are aware that שלום (*shalom*) means "*peace.*" They are also aware that שלום (*Shalom!*) is the way Israelis say "Hello," and

"Goodbye." When Israelis meet, they greet others with שלום (*Shalom!*) – "*Peace!*" And when they part, their last word to each other is שלום (*Shalom!*) – "*Peace!*"

When Jesus first appeared to the gathered disciples following his resurrection, he said, in Hebrew, "לכם שלום" (*shalom lechem!*) – "*Peace to you!*" (Luke 24:36; John 20:19, 21, 26). After Israelis greet each other with "*Peace!*," they will then ask how you are by saying, "מה שלומך?" (*ma shlom cha?*)—literally, "*What is your peace?*"—the שלום (*shlom*), as in Psalms 122:6, is simply the contracted pronunciation of שלום (*shalom*).

Now, Psalms 120–134 are called the Psalms of Ascent, that is, the Psalms that were recited, chanted, or sung, as Israelites made the long, slow journey from their cities and villages up to Jerusalem for the appointed feasts of the LORD (see Exodus 23:14–17). Not all could comply with the command to appear at each of the three feasts of LORD, and it is possible that Joseph and Mary only took Jesus to Jerusalem for the Passover feast:

His parents went to Jerusalem every year at the Feast of the Passover (Luke 2:41).

Those who were traveling up to Jerusalem were cared for in the towns and villages along the way, in the homes of people who were not going up to the feast that year. As the travelers set out again on their journey, the hosts would say to the hosted, שאלו שלום ירושלם (*Shalu Shlom Yerushalayim!*)—literally, "*Ask the peace of Jerusalem,*" but in today's vernacular it would be, "*Say 'Hello' to Jerusalem*" for me. Perhaps this helps understand the cry of the Psalmist:

If I forget you, O Jerusalem, let my right hand forget its skill! (Psalms 137:5).

The verse of Psalms 122:6 should, therefore, read: "**Greet Jerusalem**: *may they prosper who love you.*" If the reader desires to pray for the peace of Jerusalem, he or she would be better advised to pray John's prayer at the end of Revelation: *Amen. Even so, come, Lord Jesus!*" (Revelation 22:20). Peace can only come to Jerusalem after Jesus returns to reign in his city—*the City of the Great King* (Psalms 48:2). There is no other scenario for Jerusalem.

BTW: Jerusalem is generally believed to mean "*City of Peace,*" if that is true, why has the city been sacked and destroyed ninety-one times? Why, even in 2017, Israel's enemies continue to stab or shoot Jewish inhabitants to death, or ram vehicles into groups waiting at bus and light rail stops? Could the name therefore mean something other than *City of Peace*?

    Jerusalem in Hebrew is spelt (reading right to left) ירושלים. We know that Melchizedek was **king of Salem, that is, king of peace** (Hebrews 7:2), Salem in Hebrew is שלם, and from this Jeru**salem** gets her "*peace.*" We have the end of Jerusalem's name, which means "peace," and now we look at the the first two syllables: ירו (*yearu*), which means "will see," therefore ירולשם (Jerusalem) must mean "*We shall see peace.*" And that "*peace*" will come to Jerusalem only when the Lord Jesus Christ takes up his throne there.

Dear Lord:

Your Word suggests that those that love Jerusalem will prosper; let it be so! Help us to pray against terror and evil in your holy city and may our prayers form a wall of protection around those who legally inhabit this jewel of a city. O Lord, we so much want permanent peace to come to Jerusalem, therefore we earnestly petition you to send your *only begotten Son* back that he may take up his throne and rule the peoples: *Amen. Even so, come, Lord Jesus!*" (Revelation 22:20). Amen.

You Are But A Youth

David, the son of Jesse, who became Israel's most famous king, was indeed a shepherd, but being in that occupation did not freeze him either in time or growth and keep him as a young lad like Christian tradition makes him to be.

David, in the course of keeping his father's flock of sheep, had earlier killed both lion and bear (1Samuel 17:36). In fact, when a lion took one of his lambs, David **took the lion by its beard and struck and killed it and rescued the lamb** (1Samuel 17:35). Does that sound like the action of a very young man, someone not much more than a boy?

When king Saul was tormented by an evil spirit he wanted someone who could play music and soothe him:

So Saul said to his servants, "Provide me now a man who can play well, and bring him to me."

*Then one of the servants answered and said, "Look, I have seen a son of Jesse the Bethlehemite, **who is skillful in playing, a mighty man of valor, a man of war**, prudent in speech, and a handsome person; and the LORD is with him."*

*Therefore Saul sent messengers to Jesse, and said, "Send me your son David, who is with the sheep." And Jesse took a donkey loaded with bread, a skin of wine, and a young goat, and sent them by his son David to Saul. So David came to Saul and stood before him. And he loved him greatly, and **he became his armorbearer***

(1Samuel 16:17–21).

David was taken straight from the fields where he was caring for his father's sheep, to being king Saul's **armorbearer**; all warriors of distinction had such an attendant.

An **armorbearer** was a personal servant who carried the large shield and probably other weapons for a king. His job was not only to protect the king during battles, but also to kill the wounded among those who came against the king. The *Zondervan Encyclopedia of the Bible* says: "The armor-bearers used clubs and thick swords to dispatch the enemy wounded." Now, does that sound like a job for a fresh-faced kid from the far side of beyond? We are also told in the above scripture that Saul's servant said David was "*a mighty man of valor, a man of war.*" Really? This was David before he even went against the Goliath, the giant Philistine champion with nothing but a *sling* and *five smooth stones*!

Saul was chosen as king because: *From his **shoulders upward he was taller than any of the people*** (1Samuel 9:2). Which is to say that he was exceedingly tall if he was **a full head taller** than any other person. Yet before David went to face Goliath he donned all of Saul's armor, including the helmet, the coat of mail and Saul's sword and walked about (1Samuel 17:38-39). Then we read of David:

*"I cannot go in these," he said to Saul, "because **I am not used to them**." So he took them off* (1Samuel 17:39).

The literal translation of the Hebrew is that David had not "**tested**" the armor, and the majority of English-language versions translate it this way, but I have used the *NIV* rendering *"not used to"* the armor because it gives a better sense of what David was saying.

David was simply not used to wearing armor, which included the helmet and the full coat of mail, so he took it all off again. Had David been tradition's young pre or early-teen the armor might have buckled his legs due to its great size and immense weight, but we see that David put it on and tried walking about. If David had been tradition's young youth it would have been utterly ridiculous for him to even have attempted to put the armor, the helmet, and the coat of mail tailored for a king, tailored for a tall man so much greater in height and build than David. No, David was no pimply-faced youth. He was a strong, handsome, fearless young man whom king Saul almost immediately set over the army (1Samuel 18:5), which is the majority reading of the Hebrew.

The *NIV* has it that Saul gave David *a high rank* in the army and the *NLT* has Saul making him *a commander* in his army. The majority of other translations, render it:

*And David went out and was successful wherever Saul sent him, so that **Saul set him over the men of war**. And **this was good in the sight of all the people** and also in the sight of Saul's servants* (1Samuel 18:5).

Whether David was given the actual command of the army, given a high rank in the army, or made a commander in the army, it still conclusively proves that David was no immature kid with fuzz on his face. No one in their right mind would place a young lad in command of seasoned soldiers; they would refuse to fight under such a person. We are told that David's appointment over the men of war was pleasing in the eyes of Saul's servants (1Samuel 18:5), which it would not have been had David been little more than a brash youth.

The story of the early part of David's life is merely one more example of how tradition so ably manages to bury facts under a cartload of fantasy.

Dear Lord:

Do help us to differentiate between fact and fiction by studying your word. Help us to *search the Scriptures daily* (Acts 17:11) in order to find out the facts, and help us to be diligent to present ourselves *approved* unto you, *workers who do not need to be ashamed, rightly dividing the word of truth* (2Timothy 2:15). Let not *the cares of the world choke* the life of the Son of God within us, and let not *the deceitfulness of riches, and the desires for other things entering in choke the word* (Mark 4:19) that we become unfruitful. Amen.

Christmas and the Time of the Birth of Jesus

Throughout my many years I have celebrated Christmas in England, America, Thailand, Italy, New Zealand, Israel, and The Netherlands. In Israel there is no festive air at Christmas and the only trees and tinsel to be found are in Christian Filipino and Thai caregiver homes, homes of the staff of Christian expatriate ministries, and those of thousands of Russian Israelis. (Sixty percent of Russian immigrants who came to Israel following the fall of the Soviet Union were non-Jews, they bought their papers either with money or "favors.")

The Armenians in the fabled Old City of Jerusalem celebrate Christmas, as do the Christian Arabs in East Jerusalem; between them they have the trees and tinsel, together with all the commercialization and exploitation of the Western countries from which they learned the hype. To say that most ultra-orthodox Jews "frown" on Christmas in Israel would be a gross understatement. If they were to have their way some would have the word Christmas forcibly purged from people's minds.

Most Christians never question Christmas so a little information on the subject will not go amiss.

The celebration of December 25th as the birth date of Jesus came to us from the Church of the Fourth century. It was never intended to be taken as the actual day, although somehow Church tradition and the world at large managed to establish it as a virtual fact that is not to be disputed. However, the celebration of the birth of Jesus was unknown to the Church for over three hundred years. For some seven hundred years Rome celebrated the pagan festival of "The Invincible Sun" on December 25th. With Rome's acceptance of Christianity under Constantine some Christians decided they would celebrate with a festival to "The Sun of Righteousness" (Malachi 4:2) in stark contrast to the pagan festival. And that is how we came to celebrate December 25th as the birthday of Jesus.

Santa Claus is also a name with its roots back in the Fourth century. Bishop Nicholas of Myra in modern-day Turkey loved children and cared for the needy. He became a saint, eventually, and has been known by many names, including "Sinterklaas" in Dutch, which would later become Santa Claus.

The word "Christmas" evolved from "Christ Mass," but Christmas only became popular in the 1800s when Christmas trees were imported from Germany because Charles Dickens was exerting tremendous influence with his annually published Christmas stories that began with *A Christmas Carol*. The Puritans, both in England, and New England (America) tried to have Christmas abolished, but their moves proved unpopular and Christmas survived.

Since the time of the Industrial Revolution Christmas has been developed and commercialized, and the Church's previous time of quiet reflection and preparation gave way to the feverish activity that we are all familiar with today.

There have been a number of attempts to pin down the date of our Lord's birth, and there are endless arguments as to the year he was born due to the lack of critical dating specifics such as in which year did King Herod die; which was the Census that forced Joseph and Mary to travel to Bethlehem—was it a population census or a property ownership census for taxation purposes, etc.

I am not interested in attempting to pin down the year of Jesus' birth, I am solely interested in establishing which Jewish event coincided with his birth. I am only aware of one other serious attempt to establish the time and the festival related to our Lord's birth, and this was announced by a respected brother some years ago in Jerusalem. He made it known to a very large gathering of Christians from all over the world, that Jesus was born during the Jewish festival of Succot, which roughly corresponds to the month of September on the Georgian calendar that we use today.

I was at that meeting and spoke to the brother afterwards, pointing out that he had not taken something into consideration when he made his calculations, and he promised to look into what I had told him. However, his statement had gone out to several thousands of Christians from all around the world and has since become a virtual doctrine in some parts of the Christian world.

Earth-shattering events, such as the slaying of the *Lamb of God* (Passover), the outpouring of the *Holy Spirit* (Pentecost), etc., are invariably linked to Jewish festivals or historical events. Therefore, the promised birth of

God's *Anointed One*, the *Messiah*, *Redeemer*, and *King of Israel* would surely demand to be linked to an equally momentous event.

Clues to the actual season of our Savior's birth are given throughout the Bible and in Luke's gospel we read:

*There was in the days of **Herod**, the king of Judea, a certain priest named Zacharias, **of the division of Abijah***

(Luke 1:5).

Historians argue about the year in which Herod died, but for this study it does not matter to us in which year Herod died. It does not affect the historical fact that Herod was alive when Zacharias, ***of the division of Abijah***, ministered as priest in the temple. Jesus was born approximately fourteen months after the visitation of Zacharias by the angel Gabriel. Zacharias was of ***the division of Abijah—the eighth priestly division from the beginning of the Jewish year*** (1Chronicles 24:10), and was serving in the temple when the angel Gabriel appeared to him. The Jewish year has forty-eight weeks, not fifty-two like the Georgian calendar.

The Bible informs us that the priests were divided into twenty-four courses (1Chronicles 24:18) and, obviously, each course served for two weeks of the year. The trap that our learned brother and possibly others had fallen into was to assume that the priests served for two consecutive weeks, which they did not. We establish this by a reading in 2Chronicles:

*So the Levites … were **to be on duty on the Sabbath**, with those who were **going off duty on the Sabbath***

(2Chronicles 23:8).

And Josephus, the Jewish historian who lived and wrote before, during, and after the time of Jesus, and who left us perhaps the greatest legacy of early Jewish history, commented on king David's division of the priests referred to in the above passage of scripture. In *The Antiquities of the Jews*, Book 7, Chapter 14, section 363, Josephus writes:

> ...he [David] found of these twenty-four courses ... and he ordained that **one course should minister to God eight days, from Sabbath to Sabbath** ... and this partition hath remained to this day.

The priests, therefore, did not serve two consecutive weeks, but **two individual eight-day courses** separated by twenty-three intervening courses, all of which began and ended on the Sabbath, with those priests who were going off duty ministering together with those coming on duty. Thus we can safely calculate two dates for the birth of Jesus—one date being realistic, the other somewhat improbable.

The priestly calendar began in the month of *Nisan* (often called *Aviv/Abib*):

> *On this day you are going out, in the month **Abib***
>
> (Exodus 13:4).

The month of *Nisan/Aviv/Abib* roughly corresponds to our month of April. The beginning of the year was originally the first day of *Tishrei*, which preceded Succot by some twelve days, but God changed the order of the year so that it began with *Nisan* at the time the Israelites came out of Egypt:

*Now the LORD spoke to Moses and Aaron in the land of Egypt, saying, "This month [Nisan] shall be your beginning of months; it shall be **the first month of the year** to you* (Exodus 12:1–2).

*In **the first month**, which is the month of **Nisan**…* (Esther 3:7).

Eight weeks following the commencement of *Nisan* we have the angel Gabriel's visit with Zacharias. Following Zacharias' week of temple duty his wife Elizabeth duly became pregnant:

After these days his wife Elizabeth conceived, and for five months she kept herself hidden, saying, "Thus the LORD has done for me in the days when he looked on me, to take away my reproach among people" (Luke 1:24).

In the sixth month of Elizabeth's pregnancy with John, Mary became pregnant with Jesus by the Holy Spirit:

*And it happened, when Elizabeth heard the greeting of Mary, that the babe leaped in her womb; and Elizabeth was filled with the Holy Spirit. Then she spoke out with a loud voice and said, "Blessed are you among women, and **blessed is the fruit of your womb!** But why is this granted to me, that **the mother of my Lord** should come to me? For indeed, as soon as the voice of your greeting sounded in my ears, the babe leaped in my womb for joy. Blessed is she who believed, for there will be a fulfillment of those things which were told her from the LORD* (Luke 1:41–45).

Assuming an average thirty-eight week gestation took place following conception, Mary would have either given birth at the beginning of the month of *Av*, roughly corresponding to our month of July. Or, if the angelic visitation took place on Zacharias' second term of duty, the birth would have taken place in the middle of the month of *Tevet*, which would correspond to around the end of our January. This, however, is highly unlikely because it is the coldest, wettest time of the year, often with below freezing temperatures. At that time the population would hardly be expected to travel all over the country on donkeys or on foot for the census decreed by Caesar Augustus (Luke 2:1–3).

It is also highly improbable that shepherds would remain out in the open, in the fields with their sheep (Luke 2:8)—they would be housed away from the elements as the custom is still today. According to both my study and calculations the only real *holy day* the birth can possibly coincide with is the **Ninth day of Av**, the day that both the first and second temples were destroyed. How fitting for *the Lamb of God that takes away the sin of the world* (John 1:29) to be born on the **Ninth day of Av**, the day that commemorates the destruction of the two temples that could not contain him, and which did away with the sacrificial system made obsolete by the death of Jesus on a Roman cross on Mount Moriah, the place that we know today as Calvary.

The **Ninth day of Av** (*Tisha B'Av*) is the day religious Jews fast and mourn the loss of their temples. The wearing of leather or partial leather shoes is not permitted, and they deny themselves usual comforts.

Dear Lord:
Your Word tells us that **when the fullness of the time had come, you sent forth your Son** (Galatians 4:4), which tells

us that the timing of the birth of Jesus was calculated. Following shortly after the sacrificial death of your Son, the second temple was destroyed and animal sacrifices came to an end—two great temples destroyed on the very same date hundreds of years apart. The need for another edifice to house your glory has been superseded by a temple that is built without hands, your Son Jesus *being the chief cornerstone.* Your Son's birth celebrates the end of blood sacrifice and the rise of the most glorious of all temples—the hearts and minds of all true believers. O Lord, may this temple be fully complete soon. Amen.

Ezekiel's Temple

I really had no intention of adding this topic into this little book. I have generally shied away from getting into discussions about the fourth temple, because it is one of Christianity's holiest of "sacred cows." However, I felt quite compelled by the Spirit to break my pattern of reluctance in favor of airing my personal views on the subject; my own spirit says, "Go ahead, hang yourself, it's your neck!"

The reader will already have noticed that I speak of a fourth temple, not a third temple. The reason for this is that three temples have already been built in Jerusalem: by Solomon, by Zerubbabel, and by Herod. Therefore, the Church is waiting for a fourth temple, not a third. In a departure from previous chapter writings I will use quotations from existing works penned by learned men to back up my argument and to establish it. These lettered erudite men explain things in such a way and in such words that I can only wish to attain to.

First century historian Josephus, in his *Antiquities of the Jews*—Book 15 / Chapter 11, records that Herod did not **extend** the second temple, but **completely removed** the edifice built in the days of Cyrus and Darius, who had themselves determined the temple's lowly measurements. Josephus records that the Jews were fearful of Herod pulling down the existing edifice without being able to bring about the temple's rebuilding. Herod subsequently gave the Jews his word that he would not pull down the current structure until everything was ready to rebuild and on site, which is exactly what took place.

The Works of Josephus, translated by William Whiston (1667–1752) was first published in 1736. The *Complete and Unabridged New Updated Edition* of *The Works of Josephus* (1987) contains Whiston's slightly archaic original notes. Concerning Herod's rebuilding of the temple, Whiston writes:

We may here observe, that **the fancy of the modern Jews, in calling this temple, which was really the third of their temples, the second temple, followed so long by later Christians, seems to be without any solid foundation.** The reason why the Christians here follow the Jews is because of the prophecy of Haggai (2:6, 9), which they expound of the Messiah's coming to the second of Zorobabel's (*sic*) temple, of which they suppose this of Herod to be only a continuation, which is meant, I think, of his coming to **the fourth and last temple**, or to that future, largest, and most glorious one, described by Ezekiel; whence I take the former notion, how general soever, to be a great mistake.

So now it has been established that Herod did indeed remove the second temple completely in order to build a third and more glorious edifice. Consequently, I will continue to refer to the expectation of a further temple as being the expectation of a fourth temple. The matter of Haggai's prophecy will be addressed later.

I opined in the previous chapter—before there was any thought of writing about the fourth temple—that the birth of Jesus Christ coincided with the *Ninth day of Av*, the day that commemorates the destruction of the two temples (Solomon's and Herod's). Therefore, I now opine that it would be rather absurd for yet another temple to be built when God, in his divine wisdom, had both great temples destroyed on the very same day, albeit centuries apart, and chose that fateful day for the birth of his only begotten Son: *when the set time had fully come God sent forth His Son* (Galatians 4:4). Therefore, the need for a house for God's name, which he consecrated to his name (1Kings 9:7), has, in my opinion, been superseded for the past two millenniums, because God now dwells in his people. We, in both fact and also reality, are the temple of the living God:

*Do you not know that **you yourselves are God's temple** and that God's Spirit **dwells** in your midst?*
(1Corinthians 3:16).

*For **you are the temple of the living God. As God has said:***

*"**I will dwell in them**, and walk among them. I will be their God, and they shall be my people"*
(2Corinthians 6:16).

*Now, therefore, you are no longer strangers and foreigners, but fellow citizens with the saints and members of the household of God, having been built on the foundation of the apostles and prophets, **Jesus Christ Himself being the chief cornerstone, in whom the whole building, being fitted together, grows into a holy temple** in the Lord, in whom you also are being built together for **a dwelling place of God in the Spirit*** (Ephesians 2:19–22).

In addition to the above we should take into consideration some things the knowledgeable writer of Hebrews says; they give us deeper insight into God's preordained plan both for the temple and also for our salvation:

*...the Holy Spirit indicating this, that **the way into the holy place was not yet made manifest while the first tabernacle was still standing**. It was **symbolic** for the present time ...* (Hebrews 9:8–9a).

The temple of Herod was foreordained to be destroyed. It was merely *symbolic* of what was to come, and while it still stood the access way for us to enter as priests into the holy of holies was not open. But through the sacrificial atoning death of Jesus the way into the holy of holies was thrown open; however, it was not an earthly temple, it was the greater and more perfect tabernacle not made with hands, which is, of course, the Church:

*But Christ came as High Priest of the good things to come, with **the greater and more perfect tabernacle not made with hands, that is, not of this creation*** (Hebrews 9:11).

Having said that God foreordained the physical temple (a **shadow** of what was to come) needed to be **removed in order for the temple not made with hands to be established**, we must needs now turn our attention to the reason for description of the temple and the holy districts outlined for us by the prophet Ezekiel in Chapters 40 through 45.

The first point we need to digest is that Solomon's magnificent temple (described twice, in 1Kings 6–7, and in 2Chronicles 2–5) only has its measurements delineated **twenty-two** times, whereas the measurements of Ezekiel's temple are delineated **one hundred and ten** times, a very substantial difference that should be well noted for it tells us a great deal about Ezekiel's vision.

The second point that we should note is that Ezekiel is in exile in Babylon along with almost the entire surviving remnant of Judah. However, Ezekiel is commanded by a heavenly man, whose appearance was like the appearance of bronze, to tell the whole house of Israel **everything** that is shown to him concerning **the temple, the holy districts** for the priests, and **how the land was to be divided** between the twelve tribes of Israel:

And the Man said to me, "Son of man, **look with your eyes and hear with your ears, and fix your mind on everything I show you;** *for you were brought here so that I might show them to you.* **Declare to the house of Israel everything you see"** (Ezekiel 40:4).

Judah's exile from the land had been set at seventy years:

For thus says the Lord: **After seventy years are completed at Babylon,** *I will visit you and perform My good word toward you, and cause you to return to this place*
(Jeremiah 29:10).

We are told that Ezekiel's vision of the heavenly being (most likely God Almighty in a different form) was in the twenty-fifth year of the captivity (Ezekiel 40:1–3). After twenty-five years of living in exile—in the conquerer's land—the captives of Judah would most surely have lost all hope of returning home, despite the Lord having promised to take them back to their own land after seventy years.

With that in mind we can better understand the reason for the insistence of the heavenly being telling Ezekiel: *look, listen, pay attention to everything you are shown, and then tell everything that you see and hear to the house of Israel.*

At the risk of being labeled a heretic, I here state that I am of the firm opinion that Ezekiel's vision of the temple was nothing more than words of encouragement to God's chosen people. Words given by the LORD to bolster a faded hope that something better lay ahead for them; words that would help them endure a further forty-five years of captivity.

At least one distinguished commentary (*Word Biblical Commentary*) appears to uphold my opinion, at least partially, when it says:

Ezekiel's vision is **explicitly related to the exiles**: its purpose was **to crystallize the LORD's promises of restoration** given through Jeremiah.

Also consider what was written long ago by A. R. Fausset (1821–1910) for the eminent *Jamieson, Fausset, Brown* Bible commentary:

The very fact that **the whole is a vision** (Ezekiel 40:2), **not an oral face-to-face communication such as that granted to Moses** (Numbers 12:6–8), implies that **the directions are not to be understood so precisely literally** as those given to the Jewish lawgiver. **The description involves things which, taken literally, almost involve natural impossibilities**. The square of the temple, in Ezekiel 42:20, is six times as large as the circuit of the wall enclosing the old temple, and **larger than all the earthly Jerusalem**. Ezekiel gives three and a half miles and one hundred forty yards to his temple square. The boundaries of the ancient city were about two and a half miles. Again, the city in Ezekiel has an area between three or four thousand square miles, including the holy ground set apart for the prince, priests, and Levites. This is **nearly as large as the whole of Judea**

west of the Jordan. As Zion lay in the center of the ideal city, the one-half of the sacred portion extended to nearly thirty miles south of Jerusalem, that is, covered nearly the whole southern territory, which reached only to the Dead Sea (Ezekiel 47:19), and yet **five tribes were to have their inheritance on that side of Jerusalem, beyond the sacred portion** (Ezekiel 48:23–28). **Where was land to be found for them there?** A breadth of but four or five miles apiece would be left. As the boundaries of the land are given the same as under Moses, **these incongruities cannot be explained away by supposing physical changes** about to be effected in the land such as will meet **the difficulties of the purely literal interpretation.**

I will understand if some readers genuinely feel that I have betrayed the faith by expressing my views on this topic, because the fourth temple is one of the greatest of all of Christianity's "sacred cows." However, I must reiterate what I said previously, that I am of the firm opinion that Ezekiel's vision of the temple was no more than words of encouragement by God to his chosen people. Words given solely to bolster a hope that something better lay ahead for them, words that would help them to endure a further forty-five years of punitive captivity.

I believe the vast scope and size of the temple of Ezekiel's vision, in which he was commanded to *declare everything that he saw and heard*, is God's way of telling the exiles that they would not be returning to the former status quo. Every area in the temple of Ezekiel's vision is very much bigger and grander than the dimensions in Solomon's gold-encrusted temple, with the exception of the *Holy of Holies*. This area was given the same dimensions as its counterpart in Solomon's temple, because the LORD **does not change** (Malachi 3:6); he remains forever the same. Also, the division of the land between the twelve tribes remained the same as before; the only difference being that should the temple be literal, there is no area at all for several of the tribes.

Returning to the matter of Haggai's prophecy aforementioned by William Whiston, we see more anomalies that defy explanations:

For thus says the LORD *of hosts: "Once more, in a little while, I will shake heaven and earth, the sea and dry land; and I will shake all nations, so that **the treasures of all nations shall come in,** and **I will fill this house with glory**," says the* LORD *of hosts. "The **silver is mine, and the gold is mine**," says the* LORD *of hosts. "**The glory of this latter house shall be greater than the former**," says the* LORD *of hosts. "And **in this place I will give peace**," says the* LORD *of hosts* (Haggai 2:6–9).

Haggai prophesied in the period immediately following the return of the exiles from Babylon. A great many of those who returned to the now desolate and impoverished land were utterly crestfallen after seventy years of captivity. Haggai's task was to motivate them and goad them into action.

A year after the return there had been no progress insofar as rebuilding the temple was concerned; Haggai's prophetic utterances were connected to the site of Solomon's ruined temple (see above prophecy). And just as Ezekiel's vision of an enormous temple was expressly for the purpose of rejuvenating hope within the hearts of forlorn captives, so Haggai's prophecy of a greater, more magnificent temple than Solomon's, full of treasure from the nations, was for the express purpose of spuring the returned exiles into action. And the strategy worked; they shook off their lethargy and went to work. But, when the foundation was finally laid for the second temple not everyone was joyous. The elderly priests and men who had seen Solomon's temple and who recalled its grandeur wept when they saw the minuscule size of the foundations for the replacement:

But many of the priests and Levites and heads of fathers' houses, old men **who had seen the first house, wept with a loud voice when they saw the foundation of this house being laid,** *though many shouted aloud for joy, so that the people could not distinguish the sound of the joyful shout from the sound of the people's weeping* (Ezra 3:12–13a).

The second temple, built during the time of Zerubbabel's governorship of Judea was puny in comparison to Solomon's and by no stretch of the imagination can it be said that it fulfilled the LORD's words: *"***The glory of this latter house shall be greater than the former.***"* Even the glory of Herod's grand temple did not match Solomon's ediface.

We could leave Haggai's prophey there, together with my opinion that it was merely an incentive to work on the second temple, but we should dig a little deeper spiritually to see what God might be showing us here. The Hebrew text literally says that *the glory of the "**last**" – (אחרון) house – (בית) will be greater than the "first" – (ראשון).* The "***first***" house of God would be Solomon's temple, but the "***last***" house of God would be **the greater and more perfect tabernacle not made with hands, that** *is, not of this creation* (Hebrews 9:11). And the **Prince of Peace** (Isaiah 9:6) would be the **High Priest** of this house that is made without hands. Its glory will be greater than anything we can possibly imagine; *"And* **in this place I will give peace,***" says the* LORD *of hosts.*

Once again: I believe that what Christianity call Ezekiel's temple cannot be a *literal* temple any more than the glory of Zerubbabel's second temple *literally* outshone Solomon's in glory and riches. Go ahead, stone me.

Dear Lord:
Help us to be fully persuaded in our own minds what we truly believe. Help us to challenge and provoke our minds to think through what we have been taught, rather than blindly accepting something because we are too spiritually dull or lazy to search the matter out. Cause us to *search the Scriptures daily*, meditating prayerfully on all that we read. Help us to think things out and state to ourselves what we believe in order that we may share our belief convincingly with others. Amen.

Ramon Bennett, the author of this book, also writes the **Update**, the regular newsletter of the *Arm of Salvation Ministries*. The **Update** keeps readers informed on world events that affect Israel,

and also, on the ministry of Ramon Bennett and his wife, Zipporah. An annual donation of $20.00 is requested for the **Update**, which is available only by e-mail in digital PDF format. Amounts given beyond the stated amount will be put toward the personal expenses of the Bennetts. Subscriptions to the **Update** and any voluntary donations can be made via **PayPal**: <payments@ shekinahbooks.com>.

Arm of Salvation (*AOS*) was founded by Ramon Bennett in 1980 and is an indigenous Israeli ministry dependent upon gifts and the proceeds from its book and music sales to sustain its work in and for Israel and the Jewish people. These are critical times for Israel so financial support is both needful and appreciated.

Copies of **Apples of Gold** and other books authored by Ramon Bennett (see following pages) are all available on our website.

Albums of popular Hebrew worship songs composed by Zipporah Bennett, are available by making contact with Zipporah Bennett at the following e-mail address: <usa@shekinahbooks.com>.

Visit our website: *http://**www.shekinahbooks.com*** to subscribe, and/or donate via **PayPal**.

SHEKINAH

new 2015 fourth edition

*"**WHEN DAY & NIGHT CEASE** is the most comprehensive, factual and informative book on Israel—past, present and future. If you want a true picture of how Israel is falling into Bible prophecy today, look no further. You will want to read this book"*

324 pages – Paperback, or Kindle e-book

updated 2016!

PHILISTINE lays bare the Arab mind, Islam, the Koran, the United Nations, the news media, rewritten history, and the Israeli-PLO peace accord. ***PHILISTINE*** will grip you. ***PHILISTINE*** will inform you. Philistine will shock you. Until you read ***PHILISTINE*** you will never understand the Middle East—the world's most volatile region.

364 pages – Paperback, or Kindle e-book

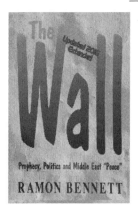

updated 2016 extended

*"**They lead My people astray**, saying 'Peace!' when there is no peace, and because, when a flimsy wall is built, they cover it with whitewash"* (Ezekiel 13:10).

    In ***The Wall*** Ramon Bennett exposes the peace process for what it is, an attempt to break Israel down "piece" by "piece." This book contains information the mainstream news media, the CIA, the White House, and others would rather you did not know.

367 pages – Paperback, or Kindle e-book

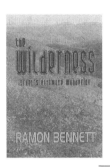

THE WILDERNESS

*"**VERY INFORMATIVE BOOK FOR THOSE WHO** are looking for answers to what is happening in the middle east. Most of what you hear in the news media is such surface stuff and news to steer you away from the truth. God's Word is truth and Ramon Bennett breaks down verses that I've wondered about for years. A very good read, you won't be able to put it down."* — William D. Douglas

335 pages – Paperback, or Kindle e-book

GAZA! is an accurate account of the events that led up to, and took place during, Israel's Operation Protective Edge, the 50-day war against Hamas in Gaza in 2014. It is a factual account of what took place, when it took place, why it took place, and the result of it having taken place.

This book gives a proper perspective—differing to what was presented on television screens across the world; it gives a different narrative to that told by Hamas-threatened journalists who covered the third round of this never-ending conflict.

134 pages – Paperback, or Kindle e-book

ALL MY TEARS – an autobiography

RAMON BENNETT has been introduced as "someone who has suffered the trials of Job."

Often verging on the unbelievable, **ALL MY TEARS** is Ramon's astounding autobiographical testimony; a story of an unwanted, abused child whom God adopted and anointed, and uses for His glory.

448 pages – Paperback, or Kindle e-book

HISTORY, the gospels of Matthew, Mark, Luke, and John blended together into a single uninterrupted narrative. **HISTORY** transforms the four individual gospels, each with its own color text, into an edifying read for those interested in the full, uninterrupted story of the nativity, life, death, resurrection, and ascension of Jesus Christ. The **Color Print Edition** shows from where each interpolated piece comes from. Bible Students find this book fascinating. Black Print Edition also available.

184 pages – Paperback, or Kindle e-book

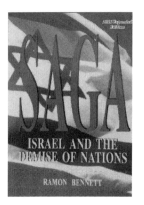

updated 2016 extended

UNDERSTAND the chaos taking place around the world today! **SAGA** shows that Jews died because cruelty and evil and anti-Semitism are not confined to one race or nation but are found everywhere. **SAGA** is about Israel and Israel's God; about war and judgment—past, present, and future. Nations came and went, empires rose and fell; and God is still judging nations today. A "must read" in light of world events today.

284 pages – Paperback, or Kindle e-book

Abe: Abraham is called the friend of God, being mentioned hundreds of times in connection with faith. Follow Abraham as he journeys to and in the land of Canaan. Be there when Abraham makes leaps of faith and the author causes us to understand why Abraham came to be known as God's friend and the Father of our Faith.

David, Israel's great warrior king, *served God's purpose in his own generation* (Acts 13:36), but Abraham has served God's purpose in every generation.

62 pages – Paperback, or Kindle e-book

My Cup Runneth Over is a call to arms! The Western Church stands at a crossroads, it is dying for lack of zeal and love for Jesus. Materialism and lust for "things" are choking it.

All-too-comfortable Christians profess to believe in Jesus, but deny Him by their silence and passivity. The Church must return to 1st-Century basics like faith and belief in a miracle working God. Effective faith results from absolute conviction.

72 pages – Paperback, or Kindle e-book

Return, Daughter of Zion! Zipporah Bennett's testimony and autobiography. Read how Zipporah, a God-hungry Orthodox Jewish girl, found the Reality she longed for. This book, often amusing, will help the reader better understand the way Jewish people think and feel about the "Christian" Jesus.

137 pages – Paperback, or Kindle e-book

Available on *Amazon.com*

Hebrew worship from one of Israel's foremost composers of
Messianic worship songs

Hallelu	*Kuma Adonai*	*Mi Ha'amin?*

"Hallelu" – Dual Hebrew–English songs of worship	*"Arise O Lord!"* Songs of warfare and worship	*"Who Hath Believed?"* Hebrew and Aramaic prophecies in song

For a descriptive overview or **to purchase the above CD albums** go to:
http://www.shekinahbooks.com

Notes

Notes

Made in the USA
Monee, IL
07 April 2021